THE MIRACLE AHEAD

The Miracle Ahead

By GEORGE GALLUP

HARPER & ROW, PUBLISHERS

NEW YORK, EVANSTON, AND LONDON

To Ophelia
whose faith and loyalty
are boundless

Contents

	Page
The Thesis of This Book	ix

PART I

THE HUMAN BRAIN

The Tardy Attention Given the Brain	3
The Wonders of the Brain	7
The Evolution of the Brain	11
Future Evolutionary Changes	16
How Much of Our Brain Power Do We Use?	20
New Ways to Actualize Our Potential	23

PART II

THE DEVELOPMENT OF MENTAL ABILITIES

A New Look at Education	29
American and European Viewpoints Contrasted	31
American Education Appraised	34
The Influences of Education	40

Page

Training the Mind   46

> *Perception, Concentration, Organization, Objectivity, Problem Solving, Decision Making, Creativity, Training Students to Be Creative*

Facts That Educational Planning Must Recognize   72

> *The Neglect of Writing, The Neglect of Reading, The Need to Teach Students to Think Quantitatively*

The Case History Approach   85

Programmed Instruction   88

Expansion of Knowledge and Reading Speed   90

The Educational Program Envisaged   92

PART III

THE POTENTIALITIES OF COLLECTIVE EFFORT

The Opportunities   99

Unsolved Problems and Unused Talents   101

America's Local Problems   103

The Talent Available   107

Experiments in Government   111

An Experiment That Failed to Live Up to Expectations   115

The Grand Delusion   119

The Great Experiment   128

Problem Solving by Group Action   132

The Shortcomings of Conferences and Similar Gatherings   137

Royal Commissions of Inquiry   140

A New Way to Solve National Problems   144

PART IV   *Page*

THE NEW METHODOLOGY

The Importance of Methodology   153
A New Method for Solving Old Problems   163
Health, Happiness, and Long Life   166
How the New Procedure Was Used to Shed Light
   on a Disease   168
Factors Contributing to Long Life   175
Factors Relating to Happiness   182
Problems That Computers Can Help to Solve   186
Industrial Disease   189

PART V

ACCELERATING CHANGE

Change and the Future   195
Preparing for Change   199
Conclusion   203

Bibliography   205

The Thesis of This Book

The thesis of this book can be stated briefly.

Man has been inexplicably slow in recognizing the greatness of his brain. Throughout the ages he has made little use of its capacities, and even at the present stage of Western civilization he vastly underestimates its potentialities.

At the same time, there is no need to decry man's current progress. Modern man has every right to take pride in his achievements, particularly in the field of science, just as Renaissance man could take pride in his art and literature. Yet there is good reason to believe that mankind can make another great forward stride, not unlike that of the Greco-Roman period, through the more effective use of his mental powers.

Obviously there is no easy or magical way to accomplish such a tremendous feat. Primarily the problem is one of learning how to utilize to a far greater extent man's intellectual equipment, individually and collectively, and of devising new approaches to the solution of the many problems that confront mankind. Further study of the brain itself and the marvels it performs should help to utilize more fully its seemingly limitless powers.

At every point in history man has assumed that civilization has reached its zenith. He has smugly refused to place himself on a scale of time that reaches thousands and millions of years into the future as well as into the past. Looked at from the vantage point of eight thousand years hence—approximately the period of recorded history

—man's progress up to the present time may appear far less impressive than it does today.

From a biological viewpoint, man's only distinctive possession is a brain, which permits him to reason, reflect, imagine. It is his one unique endowment. If, as will be pointed out in the pages of this book, he uses but a tiny part of his higher mental capacities, the increase in the use of these powers should present no insuperable task. Man has already acquired skill in harnessing power, whether it be steam, electricity, or the atom. It is therefore reasonable and realistic to assume that he can discover ways to utilize to a far greater extent the mental powers he inherits.

Since rather few persons have had the opportunity to study anthropology or to keep informed about the latest discoveries of fossil man, the opening pages of this book provide a brief account of some of the facts and theories about the brain and its origins. The introductory pages serve another purpose: they help to establish the biological basis for the main thesis of the book, namely, that man makes but little use of his intellectual capacities.

PART I

THE HUMAN BRAIN

The Tardy Attention Given the Brain

Just why man has been so tardy in recognizing the greatness of his own brain continues to be one of the mysteries of history. The Greeks, who were committed to a life of reason and the guiding principle of "Know Thyself," should have been among the first to appreciate the wonders of the human brain. Instead, they assigned it a role inferior to the heart as the seat of the "spirit" or "soul." Aristotle, in fact, regarded the brain as a cooling device whose function was to condense the hot vapors that led from the heart. His explanation for man's superior intelligence was the efficiency with which the brain kept the heart sufficiently cool for optimal mental activity.

The Greeks, and those who followed them, paid scant attention to the brain and generally misunderstood its function. It was not until some two thousand years later that the brain began to attract the interest of students. When it did become an object of scientific curiosity, it ushered in one of the freakish periods of early medical science.

In the year 1795, a young German doctor, Franz Joseph Gall, advanced the theory that the brain and the mind were inextricably connected and that mental phenomena were the result of natural causes. Gall's unorthodox views gained wide acceptance in Vienna, and his lectures became so popular that the Austrian government took alarm. He was forbidden to propound his ideas, which were held to be contradictory to religious teachings and a threat to the morals of the people.

Gall and a student, who was later to gain almost as much fame as Gall himself—Johann Kaspar Spurzheim—left Vienna as a result of this ban and after an extensive speaking tour arrived in Paris, where they were awarded attention and honors. The new field of knowledge embracing Gall's theories was called "phrenology," or the science of the mind. Interest in this subject became so widespread that phrenological societies blossomed in leading cities of Europe and the United States.

Until the time of the phrenologists, the medical profession had paid so little attention to the brain that most doctors were wholly ignorant of its structure and functions. To build credence for their theories, both Gall and Spurzheim became expert in dissection of the human brain in the presence of large audiences. If they had been content with drawing conclusions as a result of close examination of the structure and the fibrous nature of brain matter, both Gall and Spurzheim might have achieved fame as scientists. They were not satisfied, however, with describing the brain as revealed by their scalpels. Their dissection of the brain was merely a stratagem to prove theories arrived at by a priori reasoning on the part of Gall, who had early made up his mind that the brain was divided into some thirty-seven faculties, each located in a different but specific area of the brain. The development of each faculty, Gall maintained, could be determined by a close examination of the contours of the skull. The personality or character of any person could thus be revealed by studying the size and shape of his skull and by noting any peculiarities of the cranium.

In due time phrenological claims came under scientific scrutiny, with the inevitable result that their basic tenets were "murdered by a gang of facts." Areas of the brain that had been carefully marked out and delineated by such terms as "acquisitiviness," "hope," "parental love," "veneration," "amativeness," "self-esteem," and the like were, on occasion, removed by surgery or destroyed by accident or disease without apparent change in the behavior or personality of the patient. The bumps on the head were found to have no relationship whatsoever to the presumed faculty that lay underneath. When the claims of the phrenologists failed to meet the tests to which they were put, the movement fell into disrepute.

Equally important in the downfall of this pseudo-science was the horde of practitioners it spawned. Many unscrupulous followers made their living by going from town to town to examine the skulls of willing dupes and offer "character analyses" and vocational guidance on the basis of head measurements.

The abortive attempt to discover more about the brain and its functions through phrenology had important repercussions on this whole field of study. In fact, the reaction to phrenology was so violent that the human brain ceased to be an important object of study and investigation for many decades. Until fairly recent times psychologists were afraid to give too much attention to the brain, lest in some manner this interest link them to phrenology. Physiologists and biologists likewise approached the subject warily.

It was not until a hundred years after the phrenologist movement had gained wide acceptance that a new breed of scientist—the neurophysiologist and the neurosurgeon—began to study the brain in a thoroughly scientific manner. When they did, there was a paucity of established fact upon which to build. This was so marked that one of the leaders in the field, Dr. W. Grey Walter, could quote an eminent physiologist as saying as late as 1946, "It remains sadly true that most of our present understanding of mind would remain as valid and useful if, for all we knew, the cranium were stuffed with cotton wadding."

In recent years a stimulus to the study of the brain and its functioning has come from an entirely new direction. Electronic computers, with their ingenious ways of storing data and resolving simple problems, parallel the workings of the brain in some respects —certainly enough to indicate that if man can gain a greater insight into how the brain operates, this knowledge may, in turn, be useful in building even more efficient machines.

The giant computer, with the improvements that are certain to be made in the future, is destined to play an all-important role in the world of tomorrow. There is little likelihood, however, that machines will ever be able to outperform the brain except for certain specific and limited tasks. They will never attain the tremendous reach of imagination and creativity that mark the mind of man.

In a sense, this greatest tool that man has so far devised serves best to highlight the real greatness of its master and inventor.

The Wonders of the Brain

The brain of man has invented the instruments and developed the technology that reveal to us an infinitely immense universe composed of infinitely small particles. In turn, all of this has been made possible by a brain that is infinitely complex.

Some idea of the complexity of the brain can be gained from a description provided by a noted neurophysiologist, Dr. Ralph Waldo Gerard: "The units of the nervous system are the neurons, individual microscopic cells. . . . There are over ten billion neurons in the human brain, and each of the larger ones has an average of more than ten thousand connections—synapses—from other neurons! The possible number of network patterns that could be formed, or paths that nerve impulses might travel, is far greater than the total number of material particles in the universe!"

Figures of such dimension lie at the edge of incomprehensibility. A few homely illustrations may serve to point out their immensity. The total number of neurons contained in the small space occupied by the brain is roughly four times the total number of inhabitants of the world! Now suppose that every person in the world could be provided with a telephone, each telephone to be connected with every other telephone in the world and each person, therefore, able to communicate with every other person. You can now get at least some idea of the capacity and the complexity of the human brain.

It is important to understand that in the development of the

7

brain more was involved than the mere multiplication of cells. As Dr. Grey Walter points out, "Not by any stretch of the imagination could our organ of imagination have evolved simply by the accumulation, one by one, or million by million, of the necessary cells with the quite mysterious diversification of them." He underscores this statement by another: "Many other bodily adjustments besides increase of space and elaboration of its own vast communications system had to be made for the most complex organ of all creation, an apparatus of such proportions and such variety of function that the giant computers with their thousands of valves are playthings beside it."

One of the standard procedures followed in science when a problem calls for a better understanding of function is to build a working model. The problem of erecting such a model of the brain, even with the smallest and cheapest conceivable midget parts, has been graphically described by Dr. Walter. Starting with the cell itself, he observes, "If the necessary chemical contents of one cell, with insulation, capacitance, and trigger mechanism, could be crowded into a quarter of a cubic inch, it would be a miracle of construction, though still gross compared with the original. To put aside the standard number of these cells—10,000 million—for one brain [would require] warehousing space of about one and a half million cubic feet."

Dr. Walter has estimated the fantastic sum that wiring connections for this model of the human brain would cost. In terms of dollars his figure represents a sum about ten million times the total national debt of the United States. Moreover, the power required to operate the model would be at least a million kilowatts, whereas the human brain runs on a mere twenty-five. These figures provide at least some conception of the proportions of the task of building a working model of the brain.

Another concept of the almost unbelievable functions performed by the brain comes from a famous brain surgeon, Dr. Wilder Penfield. In the course of his surgery, Dr. Penfield has discovered that "there is recorded in the nerve cells of the human brain a complete record of the stream of consciousness. All those things of which a man is aware at any moment of time—all the sights and sounds—are recorded in these cells."

The mechanism by which the brain makes this recording is still unknown. Possibly it may resemble a kind of wire recorder, which can imprint sight, sound, and feeling. The implications are staggering when one considers the number of conscious experiences that must be recorded each day—in fact, each waking hour—and then filed away in the mind in such a way as to make the more important and meaningful experiences quickly available and to divert the millions of others into a dead-storage limbo.

Not only must the system of filing and indexing be a marvel of efficiency, but the speed of producing cross references and highlighting the incredibly small details that bring into focus likenesses and differences in form and meaning would put to shame man's best effort to duplicate this operation by machine.

These facts about the brain, discovered by leading students of the nervous system, help to underscore the two basic points to be emphasized here. The first is that throughout history man has made little use of the brain that nature bequeathed him; the second, that he vastly underestimates its potentialities.

The greatest students of the brain and the nervous system are fully aware of the vistas that lie ahead for mankind in the fuller use of his brain power. I need quote only two: N. J. Berrill, Fellow of the Royal Society, and Dr. Ralph Waldo Gerard of the Mental Health Institute. Professor Berrill says: "A brain, even such a small and seemingly simple one as that of a bee, is infinitely complex in its intimate structure and is amazing in its performance. When, as in this case, so much can be accomplished by so little, I am astonished that the great mammalian brains do no more than they do, with all respect to our own superior achievements. It suggests, to my mind at least, that we fail to put them to their full use, that both our present brain and its possible future developments contain potentialities as yet hardly dreamt of."

Emphasizing the same point, Dr. Gerard comments, "We . . . may be about to break through into a new epoch of creativity, under-standing, and richness that could carry mankind as far beyond the present cultural level as we are now beyond that of our Cro-Magnon forebears."

The Evolution of the Brain

A backward glance into the origins of man and into the reasons he, of all the primates, happened to develop such a large and complex brain may serve to shed light on the biological changes that have brought us to our present state. This same examination of evolutionary changes should provide some inkling of what we may expect from evolutionary forces in future millennia. More particularly, this brief review will emphasize the importance of cultural evolution as opposed to biological evolution in the immediate future of *Homo sapiens.*

Trying to reconstruct the past, the prehistory, of mankind has all the fascination of a good mystery story, and the fitting of bits and pieces together into a solution is just as difficult. Each new discovery of fossil remains of early man and his apish ancestors adds to the stock of knowledge and narrows the field of debate. With the development of more accurate methods of dating fossils, artifacts, and geological periods we may look forward to a time when the history of man is based upon hard-to-disclaim facts. However, that time appears to be far off. Anthropologists and paleontologists would be the first to admit that there are all too many questions about man's beginnings that have not been, and in all likelihood will not be, solved for many years to come.

There is wide agreement on one important point. Man is a newcomer to earth. A favorite illustration cited is the following comparison with the hours of the day. If twenty-four hours are taken to

11

represent the time since life began on earth, then the advent of man happened only the last minute of the twenty-four hours, and modern man, *Homo sapiens,* blossomed forth only the last few seconds of the last minute!

Although man emerged at this last moment of history, the exact period in geological time is still a matter of considerable debate. Anthropoid apes are millions of years old. The first man-apes or near men are now believed to be the australopithecines, a tongue-twisting word, which means South African apes. These prehuman primates in many ways resembled man, but their simian characteristics outnumbered their human features. Although they walked with upright posture and their teeth approximated man's, their skulls were only slightly larger than those of apes, and in general the australopithecines resembled apes.

Geological evidence indicates that they lived about a million years ago or about the beginning of the Pleistocene period. The last of this group of primates may have been contemporaries of early man; but they, and the other man-apes who evolved during the preceding period, the Pliocene, have long since vanished from the earth.

Following the australopithecines in point of time came the group identified as the pithecanthropines, taking their name from *Pithecanthropus erectus,* discovered in Java by Eugene Dubois in 1891. Other skeletal remains found near Peking in China are usually regarded as belonging to the same genus. These early men were more man than ape and merit a hominid status not only because their brains were larger but because they knew how to use fire and to employ stone tools of a primitive kind.

Next in time came the Neanderthal group—although other fossil remains have been placed in the interval between *Pithecanthropus* and the emergence of the Neanderthal type. Many skulls of this latter group have been discovered throughout Europe, the Near East, and Africa. Neanderthal man retained many features typical of earlier and more primitive types. His skull was thick, he lacked a chin, and his forehead receded sharply. His posture was not completely erect, and all in all he appears to have been a brutish-looking creature.

Many experts believe that the Neanderthaloids represent a race that was not ancestral to *Homo sapiens,* even though they undoubtedly came from the same common stem. While this group is regarded as an aberrant sideline that became extinct during the last period of glaciation, or about fifty thousand years ago, they did have some very human qualities. The ritual burial of their dead bespeaks some form of spiritual life. There is also abundant proof that they lived a family type of existence in their caves, which offered some protection from the cold of the last glacial period.

Neanderthal man, in turn, gave way to a people who resemble Western man in virtually all respects. This group takes its name, Cro-Magnon, from a discovery of fossil remains at Cro-Magnon in southern France. They were tall, some may have been dark, and presumably most were handsome, judging from the fine facial features revealed by the skulls that have been found. The Cro-Magnons had high cranial vaults and a brain capacity not appreciably different in size from that of modern Europeans.

While the fossil record of man is not yet complete, as Le Gros Clark of the British Museum of Natural History points out, it is sufficient to allow us to link one evolutionary stage with another in a natural sequence. Nevertheless, this record leaves still hidden in the haze of predawn history the answers to many important questions.

When did ape man cross the line and become more man than ape? At what point in his evolution did man become conscious of himself? According to Pierre Teilhard de Chardin, this was the critical point in man's evolutionary history. He points out: "Admittedly the animal knows. But it cannot know that it knows; that is quite certain. If it could, it would long ago have multiplied its inventions and developed a system of internal constructions that could not have escaped our observation. In consequence it is denied access to a whole domain of reality in which we can move freely. We are separated by a chasm—or a threshold—which it cannot cross."

Another question that remains unanswered is why the brain of man expanded so rapidly within such a short period of geological time. What evolutionary forces brought about this expansion? Adaptation, genetic alteration, and isolation are regarded as the major forces producing evolutionary change, but none of these provides a satisfactory answer to man's big brain. Most students agree with Clark that increase in brain size was first favored or accelerated by the conditions of existence associated with an arboreal mode of life. Since, however, the greatest expansion occurred long after the arboreal stage—during the four great periods of glaciation of the Pleistocene, or roughly the last half-million years—it is hard to explain how a larger brain gave its possessor any marked advantage over his less intelligent brothers in the kind of existence that must have been true of the period. At that point in prehistory man lived by hunting and food-gathering. Natural selection would almost certainly have favored the physically rugged, the fleet of foot, the fiercely aggressive.

It is most difficult to understand why, at this point in man's evolution, he should be equipped with a brain capable of performing intellectual feats of the highest order when there was no conceivable need or use at the time for these mental powers—at least no more than a Hottentot would have for a modern computer. Need does not seem to explain why these powers came into being—and certainly there is no evidence whatsoever of early man's use of his higher mental powers.

Indeed, the most perplexing aspect of man's prehistory is the incredibly long time, the hundreds of thousands of years, that it took him to learn how to make even the very simplest improvements in the stone tools he used. Later in history, primitive man learned to make fire, and throughout this latter period he must have had a simple spoken language. Even so, it would seem that the smaller brain with which he started the last half-million years would have served his needs quite adequately up to the time when he began to live in communities and practice the art of agriculture.

Still another question that has not been answered—that has, in fact, never been given the importance it merits—is the evolutionary development in present-day man of a king-size ego (which has its counterpart in nationalism and racialism in his collective life). The fierce zeal with which *Homo sapiens* protects, coddles, and inflates his ego is the dominant feature of mental life, in comparison to which sex, hunger, and other instinctive drives attain only spasmodic importance. Certainly at an early stage of our present civilization man's ego had reached its full-blown development. Why and whence came this excessive fondness for himself is just one more of the inexplicable facts not satisfactorily explained by evolutionary forces.

Future Evolutionary Changes

The search for fossil traces of prehistoric man continues with increasing zeal. New finds will inevitably bring new insights, with the result that present conclusions about the past and the probable future will undergo a continuous process of accommodation. Such has been the history of the last hundred years, since interest in evolution was awakened by Darwin's theories.

Fossil evidence is convincing that the brain of man more than doubled in size during the period of the Pleistocene. The brain cases of the australopithecines had an average capacity of 600 cubic centimeters. The *Pithecanthropus* group, which followed them in time, had a capacity of 900 cubic centimeters—which compares with an average of 1350 for modern man.

Since Neanderthal man had a skull equal in size but somewhat differently shaped from that of modern man, the expansion of man's brain must have taken place chiefly during the period marked by the first and the last glaciation, or a span of years embracing some four hundred to five hundred thousand years.

When comparisons are made with Western man, the evidence indicates little change in the actual size of the brain during the last one hundred thousand years. Changes in the brain can proceed in other respects, however. The brain can become more tightly folded or convoluted. It may undergo structural changes, although there is no positive proof that this happened. Cell connections can multiply with increased use. Nevertheless, taking full account of the possibility of internal changes, the over-all conclusion seems warranted

16

that there has been no significant change in either the size or the structure of the brain for many thousands of years.

In *The Phenomenon of Man,* Pierre Teilhard de Chardin advances a number of novel and penetrating views about the past and the future of man. Holding that the brain is the end product of all evolution, Pierre Teilhard states his belief that biological evolution has come to an end and that evolution in the future, insofar as man is concerned, will be confined largely to cultural rather than to genetic change.

Human society itself takes on the characteristics of an organism and evolves in much the same manner, in Teilhard's opinion. As proof, he says: "In the course of a few generations all sorts of economic and cultural links have been forged around us and they are multiplying in geometric progression. Nowadays, over and above the bread which to simple Neolithic man symbolized food, each man demands his daily ration of iron, copper and cotton, of electricity, oil and radium, of discoveries, of the cinema and of international news. It is no longer a simple field, however big, but the whole earth which is required to nourish each one of us. If words have any meaning, is this not like some great body which is being born—with its limbs, its nervous system, its perceptive organs, its memory."

In increasing numbers and with increasing complexity, human society will become more and more mental, a situation that is destined in the eyes of Teilhard to guide mankind to higher and higher levels of hominisation. Further, he makes the point that since "evolution is an ascent towards consciousness . . . therefore, it should culminate forwards in some sort of supreme consciousness."

The forces of life, cultural and biological, are converging upon a point that Teilhard identifies as Omega, a point far distant in time. "Life," he says, "still has before it long periods of geological time in which to develop. Moreover, in its thinking form, it still shows every sign of an energy in full expansion. On the other hand, compared with the zoological layers which preceded it whose average duration is at least in the order of eighty million years, mankind is so young that it could almost be called new-born."

Bearing in mind that any generalizations in respect to the evolutionary process are subject to questioning, it may be useful to point out areas of general agreement at the present time, particularly as they concern the brain of man. We can then take a look at what the future may have in store. With the foregoing qualification in mind, several conclusions seem warranted:

First, the brain of man will almost certainly be different a million years from now. Whether it will differ as much from the present as our brain differs from that of early Pleistocene days is a matter of sheer speculation. One can take the point of view of Teilhard that biological evolution has come to an end and that evolution will be confined to the cultural or psychosocial areas of life. Or one can agree with those who hold that changes of a minuscule order are probably occurring all the time in brain size and brain structure. Both groups, however, would caution that change comes with glacial slowness. Even a period of eight thousand years—the period of recorded history—is too short a time for any changes to become apparent. Summing up, then, we can conclude with some certainty that any changes brought about by the natural processes of evolution will not be apparent for many millennia.

Second, a nuclear holocaust might bring about radical changes abruptly by altering the genetical structure of man. Indeed, radiation might destroy the entire human race. At the other extreme there is a rare chance that a superman might emerge with a set of genes that is inheritable. Moreover, it is within the realms of possibility that man himself might at some future time try to direct his own evolution through selective breeding and artificially induced mutations. But the odds against man-made changes, by design or accident, seem sufficiently remote to remove them from present calculations.

Third, the emergence of man's brain with its unique qualities has been by far the most important evolutionary event in world history. The growing complexity of life creates an ever increasing need for the exercise of man's higher intellectual abilities. Biological changes of an important order may or may not be in store for man, but it is virtually certain that evolution of a cultural or psychosocial nature will accelerate.

Fourth, in view of what is known about the human brain, it is idle to argue whether one race is actually superior to another. Men of all races, including those of the West, use such a tiny part of their total intellectual equipment that it remains within the province of any race or nation, large or small, advanced or backward according to present standards, to thrust far ahead of other nations if it makes any systematic effort directed toward the better use of this equipment.

We return again to our basic thesis, namely, that even at our present level of civilization mankind makes use of only a small part of his higher mental powers. The potentialities inherent in the greater use of these abilities are awe-inspiring. We need not wait for nature or man's attempt to improve upon nature to lift us to a higher level of civilization; nor must we rely upon psychosocial forces to accomplish this end. The answer is to be found in man's present brain and its more effective training and utilization.

How Much of Our Brain Power
Do We Use?

The full development of the frontal lobes came in recent times, geologically speaking, and oddly enough at a time in man's history when the need for and the use of this forebrain seems to have been minimal. The new brain has enabled man to look ahead, rather than backward. It has given him the ability to imagine, to create, to plan, and to reason.

The question to which we must now address ourselves is how much of these higher intellectual powers modern man uses in the normal course of his existence. To what extent does he realize his potentialities?

Obviously, the amount and the kind of thinking of any single person, or group of persons, cannot be measured with exactitude. On the basis of observation and experience, however, we can make an estimate, and we can compare such an estimate with the views of experts in the field of brain function and mental life.

The estimate of those experts who have ventured a guess is that man does not use more than a tiny part of his higher brain powers. Figures most often cited range between 2 percent and 5 percent of the realizable potential. These estimates, of course, apply to the typical Western man and not to the exceptional. One can only speculate about the use of the brain by such men as Einstein, Newton, and Leonardo da Vinci.

A clear distinction must be made between "thinking" as the term is used here and the use of this word in ordinary parlance. The word will be used here to connote what is usually described as abstract thinking—and especially that thinking which is concerned with ideas. We are not concerned with the kind of thinking that is devoted to the simple details of living or is associated with the idle thoughts that crowd the stream of consciousness.

The person who examines his own intellectual life will gain some insight as to the accuracy of this low estimate of the experts if he asks himself a few questions about his own mental life. How much time does he spend planning and organizing his own future—not just trying to decide where to spend his next holiday? How many original ideas has he had—ideas not necessarily new, but new to him? What views has he himself formulated about life, about government, about education, about the future—views not borrowed from the press or from books or friends? How much time does he spend in reflection— in exploring the many facets of life above and apart from the details of day-to-day living? Turning to mental skills, can he read and absorb a book on foreign policy in one evening and then write an intelligent commentary on it the next day?

These are but a few of the questions that would certainly reveal, in the case of the typical member of modern society, the wide gulf between actuality and full potential. The simple truth is that modern man does not need to make use of his higher intellectual powers to live a normal existence. Brain surgery supplies ample evidence that an individual can even lead what seems to be a nearly normal life after the loss of part of his frontal lobes.

Human variability and adaptability, which go far toward explaining man's biological ascendance, will always operate to produce individuals who differ widely in ability. There is, moreover, no known way of equalizing man's intellectual capacities, which means that some individuals will always stand far out above the mass. The surest way of producing such great thinkers is to raise the general level from which they must spring.

It is inconceivable that we can reach a higher state of civilization without the further development of our intellectual qualities, which, after all, separate us by such a great distance from the anthropoid apes. In fact, even though we can take great satisfaction in the progress we are making in many fields, particularly in science, we have no reason to be content with our lot. Our achievements in many fields have been meager and unexciting. It can even be argued that we have fallen below the level of excellence of Renaissance days in many of the humanities.

Certainly no one will dispute the obvious truth that mankind still has not solved the problems of society, most of which lie outside the realm of technological progress. Our work is cut out for us, and only through the greater exercise of our intellectual abilities are we likely to make substantial headway during the next few generations.

New Ways to Actualize Our Potential

Suggestions on how man can make more effective use of his higher mental powers for his own benefit and the good of society must start with a searching appraisal of the present, free from ancient shibboleths. Any society that accepts the view that it has reached near perfection impedes its own progress. The first problem, then, is to look objectively at the present state of Western civilization from the vantage point of man's entire history. How much progress has been made? How well has Western society solved its problems? How much better is it than the civilizations that have gone before?

One thing is certain. Civilization does not proceed at a regular pace and in a straight line. There are great plateaus where no progress is apparent—in fact, periods when civilization seems to have slipped backward. Then, with little advance indication, comes a strong upward thrust.

Progress is often confined to a single area. It is debatable whether present-day Western civilization is on a plateau in most respects, despite great progress in one special area—that of science. Certainly a good case can be made that modern man does not use his intellectual powers to any greater extent than did the citizen of ancient Greece. He enjoys far more wealth and comfort and greater freedom from disease, yet modern man shows no evidence of being able to manage his own life with greater intelligence than did his ancient forebears. Nor does he solve the problems that face society in his day with markedly greater skill than earlier generations.

These observations relate to Western man. It is easy to forget that there are still many people inhabiting the earth today who have not reached the level of Neolithic man. Only a minority of the three billion human beings alive today could claim to have reached as high a cultural plane as that of the Greco-Roman era.

Many of the observations and proposals made in the pages that follow concern the general state of mankind. Others deal particularly with the United States and its special problems and are not applicable, therefore, to all nations—not even to those making up the group described as the West.

Our special concern is how civilization can be lifted to a new level. To accomplish this feat, suggestions have been grouped into four main categories, each of which will be dealt with at some length. A brief summary of the categories follows.

The first has to do with individual effort. A new educational philosophy is required—a plan that embraces the entire life span of the individual and which, in the earlier years, places major emphasis upon learning to use the mind as opposed to the mere memorizing of facts. In view of the "explosion of knowledge" which has taken place largely within the last three decades, one of the necessary functions of schooling must be to teach students to distinguish between the important and the unimportant. The new philosophy of education must take account of teaching machines, with the teacher freed to devote more thought to the greatest of all educational tasks —how to create and maintain the excitement inherent in the learning process.

The second category of suggestions deals with the great opportunities that can be capitalized upon through collective effort. Up to this point in history mankind has failed to make effective use of the talents of the great mass of people. In the United States, and presumably in many other nations, hundreds of millions of man-hours of mental effort go to waste each year because no serious effort has ever been made to use the collective brain power in the solution of problems at all levels—local, state, and national. Elected officials, congressional committees, and scientific groups have floundered in trying to solve many of the nation's more persistent problems, largely because they have not organized the conditions under which effective solutions can be produced. There is one notable exception. At least one great achievement of recent years, which will be described later, indicates how man, working in concert with his fellow men, can achieve wonders when conditions are properly ordered.

The third category deals with the opportunities made possible by new scientific procedures. The present scientific era was ushered in by the application of empirical methods, strongly advocated by Francis Bacon early in the seventeenth century. Methodology largely accounts for the amazing progress of physical science in the years since. New procedures are now available for use in the realm of social science—methods that are as promising for the solution or amelioration of social problems as the methods of Bacon were for problems of the natural world. The development of the electronic computer opens a whole new area of research and provides the chance to find the reasons why certain practices and institutions fail while others succeed.

The fourth category has to do with the problem of change. The goals that any society recognizes are largely constant over long periods of time. The means to achieve these goals must change as knowledge and experience accumulate and as conditions of life change. Since change is vital to a growing culture, it is important to examine all of the various resistances to change and to develop ways of overcoming these resistances. Society itself must accept most of the blame for the failure of social institutions and practices to keep abreast of new conditions of life brought about by progress in physical science. There is much evidence to prove that resistance to change is not inherent in man, and the great hope of the future is that a new point of view can be established toward the necessity for change in social and political forms and practices. In the whole history of man no single generation has been taught to understand change and to seek change. The educational program must accept this responsibility, not only to break the shackles of the past but to contribute to the mental health and advancement of the oncoming generations.

PART II

THE DEVELOPMENT OF
MENTAL ABILITIES

A New Look at Education

Education constitutes the chief difference between highly civilized and primitive man. Anthropologists have amassed convincing evidence that the mental equipment of primitive people is not appreciably different from that of the most advanced societies. Children of barbaric tribes, removed from their environment and provided the same kind of upbringing as that of children in the homes of the well educated, can and do perform at about the same mental level. This is true of individuals, and it also applies to tribes. Within the span of two generations a tribe in Indonesia, only a few years removed from cannibalism, has produced some of the best chess players in the world. A similar tribe has developed many highly competent mathematicians.

If education can thus enable people, within a few years' time, to vault over many thousands of years, people of today could leap forward many hundreds of years if it were possible to anticipate the kind of education that would have evolved at that point in the future. The challenge, therefore, is to predict the changes that will almost certainly come in the years ahead and to adopt, at the earliest possible time, those changes that seem most promising. The starting point in such an exercise must be a critical examination of the strengths and weaknesses of education today—particularly that which is representative of America and Europe, where formal education is accorded its greatest attention.

Such an appraisal should offer some insight into what is worth keeping and what should be changed or abandoned in our present educational programs. First, however, it should be pointed out that few areas of modern life have become so highly controversial as education, and any attempt at appraisal is certain to bring violent attacks from the followers of the many philosophies. Education in the future, and particularly the distant future, is less likely to arouse the passions of those who have strong convictions about present-day education. When a long-term viewpoint is established, it will be found that many broad areas of agreement exist. The differences, as so often happens, usually center about means or methods, not ends or goals.

The observations and suggestions offered here are based upon studies conducted by the writer to compare education in Europe and the United States. They are also based upon three decades of opinion and behavior research carried on continuously in the United States and some twenty other nations of the world. The products—that is to say, the graduates of the educational systems of the various major democracies of the world—have come under close scrutiny, particularly in respect to current thinking about major political, social, and economic issues of the day. The writer makes no pretense whatsoever of expert knowledge of the detailed or current views of the many protagonists of the different schools of thought in the field of education.

In any discussion of education it must be borne in mind that we are only now beginning to be dimly aware of the great potential of the human mind, and we have scarcely reached the point of recognizing that mankind must face up to the Herculean task of how best to develop the great and largely unused powers of the brain, and how best to apply these powers for the good of mankind once they are more fully developed. To ignore the revelations of recent years would be unthinkable; and to fail to take full advantage of them in designing an educational program for the future, unpardonable.

In devising a program to reduce the time lag in reaching a higher level of excellence, the starting point must be an objective appraisal of education, as it is in America and Europe.

American and European
Viewpoints Contrasted

European students spend more hours per year on their education, if account is taken of the actual amount of time spent in the classroom and on homework. Typically they read more books and write more essays. Their general level of information in major areas of knowledge is higher. This explains why students from Europe who enter American schools are usually one to two years advanced over students of their own age in the United States.

In a study of elementary and secondary education in five countries —the United States, Great Britain, France, West Germany, and Norway—other important differences were brought to light. The vast majority of European students expect to end their formal schooling at the age of eighteen or earlier. In Great Britain, for example, only two children in every one hundred say that they plan to continue their schooling until the age of twenty or over. By contrast, in the United States more than forty-four in every one hundred say that they hope to carry on their schoolwork to the age of twenty or longer. In West Germany, France, and Norway the differences are less marked, but still they are great.

The intention of children to carry on their education after high school reflects, to a great extent, the hopes of their parents. A college education has come to be regarded as the magic formula for success in the United States. An amazing proportion of parents (71 percent in a recent study) want their children to have a college education, and nearly as many say they are taking steps to make certain that their children will be able to carry on their education beyond the high school level.

Many reasons can be advanced to explain this difference in attitude between Europeans and Americans toward higher education. In Europe, for example, one seldom encounters the view that a university education is essential to success in life. Many young people, planning their lives, are quite content to fill humble positions.

Another reason is that Europeans do not identify education so closely with formal schooling as do Americans. Self-education plays a far more important part in the thinking of Europeans—a fact that undoubtedly explains why so many continue to read books and engage in serious study after they have finished their formal schooling. In the United States, on the contrary, education is thought of almost exclusively in terms of formal education, or "schooling." If one asks how well educated a person is, the answer almost invariably is expressed in terms of years spent in school or college.

Perhaps the most important reason why American parents so strongly desire a college education for their children is a very practical one. The relatively greater success of college graduates—as measured in terms of income and social status—is unquestionably responsible for the widely accepted view that higher education is all-important in America. For this reason parents are willing to make great sacrifices to meet the considerable and constantly increasing costs of a college education.

In Europe one finds a strong conviction that only the very bright student who has an excellent scholastic record and who can pass the most difficult examinations should attend a university. Actually, facilities do not exist there for educating scores of thousands of young people beyond the school-leaving age, which is now sixteen or seventeen in most countries. Governments do not have the resources to build institutions for many more thousands of students; and parents, in most cases, do not have the funds to send their children to institutions of higher learning.

American parents want their children to attend college regardless of their scholastic aptitude. A majority, surveys have shown, do not want colleges and universities to raise entrance requirements—largely for fear that higher standards of admission might exclude their own children from the benefits of a college education.

In defense of this attitude, it should be pointed out that the American college performs a definite function in the growing-up or maturing process. In the absence of strong home discipline and good work habits, young Americans are likely to be less mature than their European cousins. Attending college normally requires students to leave home and begin to assume greater responsibility for their own lives. In the new environment away from home they have their first brush with the realities of life and their first challenge to think seriously about themselves.

These very practical purposes served by colleges in America have had a tremendous impact upon the kind of educational system that has evolved, and they help to explain the emphasis placed upon technological and professional training as opposed to the development of mental abilities and the mastery of the major fields of human knowledge.

American Education Appraised

One way to judge any system, practice, or institution is to see how well it works. In the case of an educational system, a useful and fair method of appraisal is to examine the product in the light of the goals that the system has been designed to meet.

To do this means going directly to the graduates of the high schools and colleges of the United States to see how well they perform or measure up in specific areas. With such an objective in mind the writer organized a nationwide study, which was limited solely to graduates of American secondary schools and colleges. Before the study was undertaken, the views of leading educators were sought to ascertain the amount of agreement existing as to the goals of present-day education, especially at the higher levels. In the course of this investigation it was found that most educators agree on four basic goals.

The four goals—omitting vocational and professional training—can be summarized as follows.

1. Knowledge. To give students a background of knowledge in major areas; to acquaint them with the great developments, ideas, and events in the history of man.

2. Skills. To cultivate certain skills—particularly the ability to write, to speak, and to understand other languages, foreign and classical.

3. Citizenship. To fit students for citizenship by instructing them about government at all levels (local, state, and national), by im-

parting basic facts about the Constitution of the United States and the rights it guarantees, and by building an interest in the issues of the day.

4. Intellectual curiosity. To arouse sufficient intellectual curiosity on the part of students to induce them to carry on the process of learning throughout their adult years; to give them a greater understanding and appreciation of the liberal arts.

The study was designed specifically to provide some measure of the success of the educational system in reaching these four primary goals. Representative cross-sections of three groups were investigated: those who had finished high school, those who had spent one or more years in college after high school, and those who had been graduated from college. All age groups were properly represented—recent graduates as well as older ones. Since the study embraced the entire nation, every graduate of every high school and college had an exactly equal chance to be selected.

All the persons included in the investigation were put through a long series of questions to ascertain their knowledge in many fields and to shed light on their cultural, intellectual, and civic interests. The study sought to investigate not only the interests and knowledge of those interviewed but also the influence that their education may have had on their post-school activities.

The over-all purpose of the study was to examine the educational system, not to prove that it was either good or bad. It was undertaken in the belief that a careful testing of the product of the system would be useful to those who desire an objective appraisal of the quality of American education.

Full details of the investigation, and of the results, would fill a separate volume. Space here permits only a brief summary of the findings. As stated earlier, all persons included in the study had finished high school. To avoid confusion, the term "high school graduates," as it is used in the following pages, will refer specifically to the group that graduated from high school but did not go on to college. The term "college incomplete" will refer to those who attended college but did not graduate. At the time of the survey

(1957) some 29 million adults in the nation had finished high school; an additional 8.5 million had attended college but had left before graduation; and another 8.7 million adults had been graduated from college. Persons still in school were not included in the investigation.

The results reveal many areas of ignorance about the world, past and present. Here are a few examples. Only one high-school graduate in six (16 percent) could identify Freud correctly; more than a third of all college graduates did not know his field of distinction. Only one high-school graduate in three knew who Gainsborough was; only one in five could identify Rubens. Fewer than half of those who attended college could identify Rubens; only slightly more than half, Gainsborough. Of those who graduated from college, only 30 percent could identify Schopenhauer; only 38 percent had heard of Immanuel Kant.

Even college graduates failed to pass the simplest kind of geography test. Their lack of knowledge about nations of the world was shocking. Only a third could guess the population of Russia within a margin of error of 25 percent; and only slightly more than half had a fairly accurate idea of the population of the United States.

Lack of information about the economic system of the United States can only be described as amazing. Even among college graduates only one in five had a realistic concept of the profits that are made by American companies. Only a third of America's college graduates could cite a single advantage of its economic system over Russia's.

A third of all graduates (high school and beyond) could not name one of Russia's satellite countries in Europe. Even college graduates could name only three, on the average. Yet one in ten of this latter group could not name a single country behind the iron curtain.

The skills that the educational system hopes to improve center largely about language. Skill in language can be measured in a fairly satisfactory manner by a vocabulary test. In fact, a short vocabulary test can be substituted for an educational achievement test when time limits make impractical a longer test.

To shed some light upon the language skills of high school and college graduates, a list of eighteen words was compiled from magazine and newspaper articles. Words that can be described as tricky were excluded; only words that are frequently used were included, as the reader himself can judge. The words finally selected for the test were: obese, inane, banal, plebiscite, sagacious, plebian, nepotism, avocation, laconic, soporific, elite, nostalgia, enervate, recondite, surfeit, omnipotent, ostracize, and panegyric.

The results of this part of the investigation were most enlightening. Half of all high-school graduates of the country (those who have not gone beyond this level) could not give the meaning of more than one of the eighteen words, even when the greatest latitude was given them in their answers. Those who had finished high school and spent one or more years in college could, on the average, give the correct meaning of only four of the list of words; college graduates knew the meaning of only seven of the eighteen words.

In earlier generations the mark of the educated person was his ability to speak many foreign languages. With increased communication with other people of the world, new emphasis is being placed today upon the ability to speak and to read a foreign language. The requirement of foreign language study in the schools had been declining in recent decades. Many present high-school graduates were not required in their day to study a foreign language. On the other hand, most college students were required to study at least one foreign language. To find out, in a simple way, how familiar graduates are with the foreign languages included in the curricula of most high schools and colleges, the following test was devised. Each graduate was asked if he could recall the word for *sister* in any of three languages: French, Spanish, German. Of the total sample, only 5 percent knew the German word for *sister*, 9 percent the French word, and 4 percent the Spanish word. Surprisingly, two thirds of all college graduates could not recall the correct word in any one of the three languages.

Every authority on democratic government has stressed the importance of an informed citizenry. To vote intelligently, voters must know something about the important issues of the day and the views of the nation's political leaders. Voters should obviously have some understanding of the structure of their government. They should take an active part in the democratic process. Government should not be left to others, and certainly it must not be left to the ignorant.

The chief justification for spending many billions of public funds to support free public education and subsidize colleges and universities is the need for an informed and active citizenry. If those who receive this free education do not respond by taking an active part in the political process, government must inevitably fall into the hands of smaller groups, whose self-interest encourages and permits them to gain control.

If individuals are to be fitted for citizenship by the educational process, this must be accomplished in the secondary schools. More than eight out of ten young people attend high school; fewer than half of those who come of voting age have had the benefits of college training. It is, therefore, imperative to see that high school students are properly informed and motivated, with the goal of making them effective citizens when they have finished their schooling and reached voting age.

Results of the study of high school and college graduates raises genuine doubts as to the effectiveness of the present educational system in producing an informed and active electorate. For example, fewer than half of all high-school graduates, including those who had gone to college, could name the senators of their state; fewer than half could name the representative in Congress from their own district. At the time of the investigation fewer than half of all graduates could name the Chief Justice of the Supreme Court. Only half knew that elections for seats in the House of Representatives are held every two years; only half knew what the Bill of Rights is.

No single test, including the one reported here, can provide an all-inclusive appraisal of our educational system, even though it is applied to the product of that system. Enough data can be obtained, nevertheless, to arrive at a judgment of the effectiveness of the system. From the facts, the conclusion would almost certainly be that the educational system of the United States has not been notably successful in imparting basic information in major areas of learning. Knowledge is one test; behavior is another. In the following pages more details are provided to indicate the influence American education exerts on the behavior of graduates. Results are reported on "what they do" in contrast to "what they know." The facts shed even more light on the strengths and weaknesses of the type of education that has developed in the United States.

The Influences of Education

A good case can be made for the view that the chief goal of formal education should be to arouse the intellectual curiosity of students. The years after college add up to about fifty, on the basis of present longevity figures, and it is these fifty years of adult life that education can and should profoundly influence.

If education is regarded as something limited to the early years of life—if it is associated closely with formal schooling, as it so often is in the United States—then its influence on the lives of graduates is likely to be minimal and disappointing.

William Graham Sumner made a sage observation many years ago when he said: "The great American dream is universal education. The great American tragedy is that education is confused with schooling."

Because education is so completely identified with schooling in the United States, the whole field of self-education is neglected. As soon as students receive their diplomas and degrees, there is a strong inclination to assume that they are "educated" and consequently need not bother thereafter to follow any program of serious study to further their intellectual growth. Sir Richard Livingstone of Oxford University once described the view that systematic education ends with the acquirement of a college degree as "monstrous." He said, "Who can suppose that spiritual and intellectual growth ceases and knowledge and wisdom are finally achieved when a university degree is taken, or that the need of knowledge does not grow more urgent with the passing of the years?"

With the rapid expansion of knowledge in every field, it becomes even more necessary to turn to self-education during the years following graduation. There is no other way to keep up with the vast outpouring of facts and no other way to meet fully the responsibilities of an informed citizen in a democratic nation.

Some recognition of the need to carry on the process of learning throughout life is evidenced by the development of adult education programs. Admirable though they may be in purpose, however, these courses fall far short of providing a systematic and comprehensive lifetime program. The practical and vocational courses—typewriting, shorthand, dog training, ballroom dancing, home decorating, swimming, and the like—can only be described as educational if this word is interpreted in its broadest sense. Actually, the number who enroll in educational courses intended to advance intellectual growth and understanding is disappointingly small.

The most recent figures corroborate data collected earlier. In an investigation conducted by the National Opinion Research Center, a total of 16 percent of the adult population were found to have taken part in some type of adult education program during the previous year. Of this total only a small minority had enrolled in courses that had any substantial intellectual content.

Individuals can further their cultural development in many ways other than enrolling in organized adult education courses. Many follow their own program of reading or study at home; others attend lectures and concerts or visit museums and art galleries. In the investigation of high school and college graduates described earlier, it was found that only one in fourteen of all high-school graduates (7 percent) had taken part in any type of course, lecture series, discussion group, or self-planned program of cultural improvement during the previous year. The comparable figure for the group that had gone beyond high school in their education but had not graduated from college was 18 percent. For college graduates the figure was 23 percent.

Even more enlightening are the figures on the reading of books. Exactly half of the high-school graduate group said that they had not read a book during the previous year. Nearly half (46 percent) of those who had attended college but had not finished their college work had not read a book during the same period. A third of those who had obtained their college degrees had not read a book all the way through during the previous year. These figures give small comfort to those who defend the present system of education in America.

In fact, an excellent case can be made for regarding the reading of books as the best over-all index of intellectual interest and cultural development. Groups can be compared on this basis—even nations. The United States has the highest level of formal education of all nations of the world—that is to say, students spend more years in school and a higher proportion go on to college. Nearly half of all adults in the nation have had the advantage of a high school education or better. Yet when comparisons are made of the book-reading habits of the United States with those of Great Britain, France, Germany, Holland, Switzerland, and the Scandinavian countries, the United States emerges at the bottom of the list.

In the most recent study (1963) nearly two-thirds of all adults in a representative sample of citizens of the United States reported that they had not read a book all the way through during the previous year (excluding the Bible and textbooks). Only one adult in six, in this same study, could think of any recently published book he would especially like to read. Other and more detailed findings about book reading will be offered later, when problems connected with interest in reading are discussed at length.

This same lack of interest in serious material is reflected in the studies of newspaper-reading habits that have been carried on for the last three decades. As the over-all educational level of America rises, those newspapers that devote more space to national and international news, as opposed to feature or "human interest" material, have made greater circulation gains than their competitors. Yet the amount of time the typical reader devotes to foreign news on a typical day is lamentably brief. In a study sponsored by the International Press Institute it was found that the typical daily newspaper in the United States prints an average of 84 column inches of international news on a typical day. Of this amount, the average reader reads 10 column inches—approximately the amount that can be read in three minutes of reading time!

The various media of communication reflect with great accuracy the cultural interests of the public. Television and radio programs are constantly checked to determine the size of the audiences they attract. (Obvious improvements can and should be made in the research services that estimate the size of these audiences, but even with their admitted failings they offer a fair approximation of audience size.) What the findings reveal about our educational system, as judged by its product, is not very encouraging. In all the years of radio and television broadcasting not one program of an informative or educational character has ever succeeded in finding its way into the top ten programs in popularity!

Examining the influence of the educational system in another area —the building of an informed and active citizenry—further weaknesses come to light. In no major democracy of the world does so small a proportion of eligible voters take the trouble to vote as in the United States. In the mid-term congressional elections fewer than half of all adults bother to cast their ballots. Even in Presidential elections fewer go to the polls than is true of European countries, where the general level of formal schooling is far lower. Many factors can influence voting, among them residence requirements, registration laws, one-party regions, and the like. Because of these factors, a better guide is the active participation in the election process itself by citizens.

In the investigation of the product of the American school system —its graduates—it was found that only one high-school graduate in twelve (8 percent) had done any work in the Presidential campaign of the previous year, for any candidate or party. Only one in eight of the college graduates (12 percent) had engaged in any type of political activity.

It would be unfair to the defenders of the present system of education in the United States not to point out that with all of its shortcomings it has had, as the figures reveal, a measurable and important effect upon the cultural development of America. Although the figures are far from impressive, more college graduates read books than do high-school graduates, and more high-school graduates read books than those who have had only elementary school educations. A higher percentage of college graduates attend symphony concerts, visit art galleries, support the legitimate theater, and exercise their right to vote than of those whose educations stopped at an earlier point.

American education is unquestionably at its very best in the field of technical and professional training. The standing of the United States in scientific and professional areas is second to none. The quality of scientific research undertaken in the graduate colleges of American universities has brought high praise from educators throughout the world. Moreover, such training opportunities are open to the many, not to the few.

These accomplishments must be put down on the plus side of the ledger. But if great improvement is to be made in American education, we must examine carefully the minus side. Here we see that the evidence points strongly to the conclusion that the typical product of our schools sees little necessity and little reward for furthering his intellectual growth once he has finished with formal schooling. While he is deeply convinced of the importance of education, his interest all too often does not extend beyond the vocational aspects of schooling and the better jobs with higher salaries and greater prestige that this type of training makes possible.

Rather few Americans would accept the dictum laid down by Schopenhauer over a century ago. He wrote: "No difference of rank, position, or birth, is so great as the gulf that separates the countless millions who use their heads only in the service of their bellies—and those very few and rare persons who have the courage to say: 'No, it is too good for that; my head shall be active only in its own service; it shall try to comprehend the wondrous and varied spectacle of the world' ... These are the truly noble, the real noblesse of the world."

One need not take this extreme position of Schopenhauer's or, on the other hand, the position of those who think of learning solely in

THE INFLUENCES OF EDUCATION / 45

terms of its vocational aspects. Both points of view are essentially selfish and overlook the great possibilities in new types of training, which will help society solve many of its most persistent problems and will lift mankind to a higher state of civilization.

Training the Mind

The broad outlines of the kind of education that will evolve in the future can be sketched with some measure of certainty. If we have the ingenuity and the courage to adopt, in the years immediately ahead, those changes that already seem indicated, we can by this action alone reduce the cultural lag that has always impeded man's progress.

The appraisal attempted in the previous pages points to certain basic changes that can and must be made. Few can deny that present educational systems do not encourage in students a conception of education as a lifelong process. Nor is any system of public education notably successful in giving a substantial number of students a mastery of the major fields of knowledge or the essential communication skills. These are serious shortcomings; but by far the most important defect is the failure to develop to any great extent the intellectual capacities of students. Amazingly little effort is made by the educational systems of Western nations to set the mind of the student in motion—to provide him with the kind of education that will enable him to cope with new situations as they arise, help him to sharpen his critical judgments, develop more fully his creative talents, and show him how to go about producing new and better solutions to his own and society's problems.

Ironically we are now witnessing an effort on the part of some of our most highly trained experts to explore fully the potentialities of the newest computers while the potentialities of the human brain—a far greater instrument—go unheralded and largely unexplored. Only when researchers find new ways for computer systems to help solve human problems are we made aware of the far greater efficiency with which the brain deals with these and other problems.

It will always be important for students to know the great ideas, the great works, and the great events in the history of man. Nevertheless, this is not the only or even the primary objective. It is equally certain that the training of the mind itself must assume prime importance. There is no necessary conflict in these goals; in fact, they complement each other in many respects.

Strong support for the proposal to train mental functions comes from Aldous Huxley, who says the time has come to think of *training directly* the mind "that has to do the learning and the living."

Unfortunately language has done much through the ages to confuse and thwart this goal of training the mind. We speak loosely of teaching students to think—a statement that has no more meaning than to assert that students must be taught to act. The word *think* has been aptly described as a "polymorphous" concept, which covers everything from remembering to put the cat out-of-doors to constructing a new hypothesis on the nucleus of the atom. It would be far better to speak of training mental functions or abilities, although these terms are not fully descriptive of mental operations, which range all the way from being more alert to the world about us to the process of arriving at better solutions and decisions.

Many questions remain unanswered as to just which mental functions can be most effectively trained and how to go about training them. Moreover, questions arise as to the best time in the student's program to introduce such training. Nevertheless, a start must be made, and evidence is already accumulating that certain mental functions can be trained profitably. With present research techniques, even a moderate amount of attention to this aspect of education can do much to offset centuries of neglect.

Some of the mental abilities that undoubtedly can be cultivated are listed here. Afterwards each will be discussed briefly, with the intent of stimulating thought rather than making final pronouncements.

Perception. Our connection with the world—our awareness of it—comes through perception. Experiments in recent years are extremely encouraging in showing what can be done to train this mental function, and to demonstrate the beneficial effects of this training.

Concentration. Broadly speaking, mental powers are effective in proportion to the degree of concentration with which they are applied. The highest order of abstract thinking requires the greatest degree of concentration. Quite remarkable ways have been found by some races and religious sects to improve the individual's power to concentrate. These need to be examined carefully to see if they can be usefully incorporated into a training program.

Organization. One of the most important factors contributing to success in school, in business, and in daily life is the ability to organize one's ideas and efforts. Mental powers are most productive when they are systematically directed.

Objectivity. The real mark of mental maturity is the ability to look objectively at oneself, one's work, one's country, and one's time in history. Failure to develop objectivity retards both the individual and society, and produces many of our mental ills.

Problem Solving and Decision Making. The importance and the feasibility of training the individual in problem solving and decision making are widely recognized today. In his daily life each person is called upon almost hourly to solve problems and make decisions. If he could improve his ability in these two respects, the gains should be immediate and considerable.

Creativity. Many studies are being undertaken at the present time to learn more about environmental factors conducive to creativity. The process is far less mystical than earlier researchers thought. A training program can help most students to be more imaginative and creative, and the nature of such a program can now be outlined.

If the direct training of the mind is accepted as a proper goal of education, then a radical reformation of the educational system is entailed.

Huxley suggests that to discover effective ways to train the mind, foundations might help by undertaking a world-wide search to "look into all these scattered techniques for realizing desirable human potentialities—look into them, test them, see whether they work—determining the underlying principle in the various techniques, and finally formulating means by which these techniques and these principles could be applied in general education on every level, from kindergarten to graduate school."

He adds this further comment on the possible benefits of such a plan: "My own feeling is that if this were done we would find within five or ten years an enormous amount of valuable material which, if applied to our educational systems, would do a great deal to improve these systems and a great deal for the actualization of intelligence and friendliness and creativity among human beings."

Perception

The systematic training of the mind might well start with perception, that is to say, with our awareness of the world. Huxley calls attention to the experimental work of Professor Samuel Renshaw of Ohio State University, who for many years has been experimenting with ways to improve visual perception. In Huxley's words: "It has been shown that when you give children on the elementary level training in perception you do improve their intelligence: you improve their interest in what they are doing, you improve their reading, you improve their arithmetic, and because they pay more attention, you improve their behavior in school."

Training in awareness goes back many centuries. Huxley reports that in an early Sanskrit text he found a dialogue between Siva and his spouse, Parvati, on this subject. Siva offers a list of 112 exercises for developing awareness. The exercises, Huxley states, "cover every field of human experience, teaching awareness of everything from praying to sneezing to eating to making love." He adds, "It is curious that these old procedures have been completely neglected, that one can find again and again individuals or whole cultures that had developed very important techniques which were then totally neglected thereafter—but which yet retain enormous value."

Many ways have been found to improve awareness. The method employed by Professor Renshaw is a simple and direct one, built around speed of perception. Primarily it involves perceiving and reproducing digit patterns. The digits are flashed before the eyes of the student for a given number of seconds, or fractions of a second, by an instrument called a tachistoscope.

The digits might be 7 9 3 4 5 6 1 2, for example. These eight numbers are exposed in a quick flash by the machine, and the student strives to repeat them accurately. After many training periods the time required to reproduce them is reduced sharply. The number of digits exposed can, of course, be altered as the occasion requires. Professor Renshaw found that in the case of one college student 17 seconds were necessary to repeat accurately a fifteen-digit number. After some fifty practice sessions lasting twenty minutes each, this same student was able to perform the feat in 2.1 seconds. Another student reduced the time from 20 seconds to 1.45 seconds.

Professor Renshaw has experimented with many different types of persons, ranging from physicists down to six-year-old children in the public schools. The results of this type of training in visual perception have been most impressive. As measured by standard tests, they have demonstrated that "after even relatively limited digit skill is attained the indices of comprehension and speed in silent reading show marked gains." Another interesting effect of this type of training is that the visual form field of the eyes is actually enlarged.

The six-year-old children in the public schools who had been given this type of training were tested again five years later to see if the early gains had been retained. Even after a lapse of five years it was found that the children had a superiority of about a year in total achievement, about a year and a half in reading, almost as much in spelling, and a trifle more than a half-year in arithmetic. Professor Renshaw makes the point that if these children had been given the same type of training in visual perception each year, their gains would have been even more remarkable. Just as the muscles of the body are strengthened by regular exercise and use, and tend to weaken and atrophy through disuse, it must be assumed that mental operations can be improved and strengthened by a program of systematic and repeated exertion.

Awareness can be trained in other ways. A teacher of composition in a midwestern university, accepting the view that most people go through life with their eyes only half-open, held that the way to teach students to write was to teach them to see. His students were required to describe in detail such things as the houses and lawns in the block where they resided. Each week these students had to deal with an equally familiar scene.

Almost without exception the students were astonished to discover how indistinct, incomplete, and inaccurate their recollections were. In time they gained a heightened awareness of their surroundings by consciously cultivating the habit of looking. Each one, in varying degrees, increased his capacity to perceive. The success of the professor's students in the field of writing attests to the soundness of his assumption that "if you want to write, you have to learn to see."

Concentration

The statement has been made that, broadly speaking, mental powers are effective in proportion to the degree of concentration with which they are employed. In view of the fact that men make use of only a small part of their mental capacities, importance must be attached to the ability to make more efficient use of the mental functions that are brought into play.

Concentration is certainly one of the talents Aldous Huxley had in mind when he said that a world-wide search should be made to look into the various techniques that have been discovered for realizing desirable human potentialities.

The ability to concentrate can obviously be trained. In the pursuit of religious goals many cults in India have known for centuries how to develop, through exercises patiently and persistently followed, the ability to concentrate to an extraordinary degree. There is nothing secret about their training; countless books have been written on the subject.

Undoubtedly the reason why more attention has not been paid to such methods is that ends and means become so confused that the training of concentration through exercises earnestly pursued takes on the coloration of a religious observance. Because control of the mind is associated with cults, it is often looked upon as an occult art, tied up with mystical religious rites, rather than as a practical necessity in the world of today and tomorrow.

No one can deny that a few favored individuals without special training of any kind develop the ability to concentrate to a high degree. Motivation and interest are both part of the mental set that enables some persons to focus their minds on a single idea or problem for long periods, whereas others are unable to think about an abstract problem for more than a few minutes, if at all.

The basic assumption here is that *all* mental abilities or functions can be trained. Some students will respond to a much greater extent than others to any kind of training, but virtually all will show some improvement, even though it be slight.

The only question, then, that must be answered is whether such training is worth the time and the effort involved. It is the conviction of the writer that the improvement of mental functions, such as the one under consideration here, is of far greater importance in the life of the individual than the time and effort devoted to the studies that make up present educational programs.

Some educators believe that the ability to concentrate can be developed by encouraging, or requiring, students to deal with more difficult material. Their complaint is that students are rarely forced to deal with ideas of an abstruse order, that they are seldom forced to wrestle with abstractions requiring long periods of intense concentration. Since minds are never toughened, never pushed as far as they will go, many students do not acquire the mental discipline that will enable them in later life to undertake difficult mental assignments. They never get beyond the flabby stage of youth.

Whether the ability to concentrate should be developed by exercises or by the mastery of more difficult content, or by a combination of the two, is not of overriding importance. An experimental program could probably shed much light on the best procedure. What is vital is that the importance of concentration be recognized and that a start be made to improve the student's ability to concentrate, so that he may employ his mental powers to greater effect.

Organization

Can the persons who go through life without learning how to organize either their ideas or their efforts be helped by a training program in their school years?

All too often, the failure to develop this particular ability becomes confused with intelligence. The student who does poorly in his schoolwork because he has not learned how to organize his time, his thoughts, or his work is all too likely to be regarded as dull, whereas his failure should be attributed to the simple fact that he does not know how to go about his job.

Achievement in most fields is greatly facilitated by proper planning; and such planning, in turn, is a matter of organization. A few fortunate persons have no need for training in this respect. But an educational system cannot ignore the many for the few. If the goal of a democratic society is to make opportunities equally available, that society has the moral responsibility to establish the kind of educational program that makes certain that no student is handicapped for want of proper training. The goal of equal opportunity will not be realized until every individual has been developed to the full extent of his potential.

If a student has a physical handicap, every effort is understandably made to see that this does not handicap him in his schoolwork. The same point of view must obtain in the case of mental abilities. If a student does poor work because he has not learned how to organize his time, his ideas, or his task, the responsibility must rest upon the educational system to do everything possible to help him overcome this disability. Otherwise, the goal of equal opportunity becomes merely a tired shibboleth.

Far too many educators—and others, for that matter—fall into a point of view that might be described as "educational predestination." To them, students are born good or poor; and since God or biological forces made them that way, nothing can or should be done about it. The poor students, as a result, are condemned to an educational purgatory. Fate meant it to be so.

This primitive attitude hardly befits the educational system of a civilized society. The truth is that we have only very limited and questionable ways of separating the "good" from the "poor." Moreover, we know with absolute certainty that our ideas about both will undergo a radical change during the next fifty years, when we expect to know much more than we presently do about human potentials. All that we can conclude at this time is that some students are fortunate enough to have abilities that need little training; others have abilities that need a lot of training. Many of the so-called poor students of today who find it difficult or impossible to gain admittance to the better colleges and universities may be the very ones who are sought after by institutions of higher learning when more is known about the extent to which abilities can be trained and potentials realized.

Testing of specific abilities is a useful function, which will grow in importance. However, the purpose of this testing should be to guide and not to put labels on individuals that lower them in their own or others' esteem.

The pertinent question, again, is this: Can a training program be devised that will improve the student's ability to organize? As in the case of other abilities, we cannot say with finality because it has seldom been tried, at least in a systematic manner. We do know that teaching students to do such simple things as outlining helps them to organize their work. It would seem reasonable, therefore, to assume that a far more comprehensive program, which provides exercises in how to go about organizing one's time, one's thoughts, and one's efforts, would offer real help to the millions who reveal all too well by the lives they live that they need such training.

Objectivity

Can man be trained to look at himself, his work, and his times with greater objectivity? Attempts to train individuals in this type of self-appraisal have been few, which may explain why so many persons with towering intellects remain all their lives in a childlike state of immaturity insofar as their personal life is concerned.

Western man seems to have inherited an inflated ego, which all too often keeps him in a state of constant turmoil, as previously pointed out. Every trivial aspect of life related to his self-esteem upsets his mental equilibrium. Great stores of mental energy are therefore dissipated in protecting the ego from every real and imagined threat.

Is it possible, in the schooling of the young, to deal with this important aspect of mental life? Can students be taught to see themselves as others see them? Or what is more to the point, can they be taught to see themselves as others should see them? Can individuals reach a stage in their mental growth when they accept adverse criticism, or praise, for exactly what it is worth, without untoward emotional effect?

Training in self-criticism and the development of an objective viewpoint of oneself should be part of the educational program. Even a small measure of success in such training is likely to be accompanied by a great improvement in mental health and the release of mental energy for more constructive purposes.

What is required is the establishment of proper perspectives. These are essential if self-deception is to be lessened and if the ability to distinguish between the important and the unimportant in daily life is to be improved.

Failure to be objective about the period of history in which one lives can introduce errors and distortions of another kind. Robert Hutchins has pointed out that the "proconsuls of the British Empire in the nineteenth century went out with an educational equipment consisting of a thorough mastery of the language, history, and philosophy of Greece and Rome—two civilizations that were dead. It was through the study of these two high civilizations that these men . . .

were able to get outside their own civilization, outside their own structure of government, outside their own history and mark out the lines that empire should follow."

It can be argued that a proper scale of observation, in respect to time, should embrace the whole sweep of man's history and pre-history. Viewed from the vantage point of the last fifty thousand years—the period during which modern man is supposed to have appeared on the scene—events of recorded history take on an entirely different aspect. The great wars, which seem to have been turning-points in the history of civilization, shrink to little more than a need-less and stupid shedding of blood that achieved next to nothing. If one looks from the long-term viewpoint of man's entire history, there are no victors or vanquished.

Even highly civilized man has still to attain the kind of maturity that will enable him to look honestly at himself and at the society of which he is a part. A plausible reason for this situation is that he has never been taught to appraise his own weaknesses and strengths or to view his own times in proper perspective. Without benefit of this type of training, and the maturity that should grow out of it, man is buffeted about on a sea of doubts, without compass or stars to give him direction.

Problem Solving

Of all functions in the intellectual life of civilized man, none is more important than problem solving. Problems generate problems. The solution of one creates another of a higher order in an ever continuing spiral as civilization moves forward.

The expression "problem solving" is used here in its broadest sense. It includes the personal problems with which modern man is beset from the time he arises in the morning until the time he goes to bed at night. It comprises those problems met daily in the business and professional world. And it embraces the wide-ranging problems of society itself—all the political, economic, social, and scientific issues that arise in a highly organized society.

Just as there are many different kinds of problems, there are many different ways to go about solving them. If progress is to be made, then present methods must be improved and, even more important, new methods must be developed. It was undoubtedly the rational approach to problem solving employed by the Greeks that accounted in large part for the rise of Hellenic civilization; and it was the empirical approach, advocated by Francis Bacon, that introduced the present scientific era.

New approaches, almost as promising as these, now loom on the horizon. In fact, at least one, "operations research," is now being employed, chiefly in the field of business and military planning. Other new approaches offer the hope of solving, or at least alleviating, many pressing problems of a political and social nature. Because of the importance of these new approaches, they will be dealt with at some length later.

Since we are presently concerned with the training of the individual, the question must be answered as to whether or not a student's problem-solving ability can be improved by instruction, and whether he can be helped enough to justify making this type of mental training a part of the educational curriculum.

There are always those who insist that certain abilities are "natural" and need not be trained. The truth is that all abilities improve with practice and exercise, and certainly this is the case with thinking processes. We improve our mental abilities by use in very much the same way that we improve our physical abilities.

The importance of problem solving has been recognized by graduate schools of business and other institutions interested in training executives. Highly sophisticated and mathematical theories have been developed, which with the help of computers can demonstrably improve the problem-solving process.

There is no need to wait, however, until the college graduate level has been reached to begin a training program in problem solving. It can start at a much earlier stage in the education program. The training, obviously, must be of a simple and basic nature; and it should be directed particularly at those problems with which the individual must deal in his own life.

Young persons can be trained to do a better job of "thinking through" a problem, and they can acquire skill in reducing complex problems to simple ones. There is much evidence to indicate the need for such training, on the one hand, and the possibilities it will open, on the other.

During the last three decades the writer has had the opportunity to study the views of millions of persons on a multitude of issues. The thinking of adult citizens with widely varying educational backgrounds has been examined with respect to all the major issues of this period.

From this experience many conclusions can be drawn about the capacity of the general public to arrive at sound opinions. One such conclusion is that the term "emotional," often used by critics to describe the views, usually political, of the mass of citizens, is wholly inaccurate in both its psychological meaning and its practical sense. The views of the great majority of people are rational and logical, and there is much evidence to show that their collective judgments are extraordinarily sound. This does not mean, however, that individually their thinking cannot be improved. Although logical, all too often the thinking of the individual does not go far enough; it fails to go beyond a first or second stage of analysis, as will be pointed out. And all too often the typical citizen displays far too much timidity in his thinking about problems of the day, especially those problems that look far more difficult than they actually are. Instruction, therefore, is needed to overcome this reluctance to deal with so-called big problems and to show the student, and the citizen, how even the most complex and abstruse problems can be reduced to simple and manageable components.

Improvement in problem solving can be brought about by training the student to carry the process of analysis at least one stage farther than he normally would. The following example will illustrate the steps in this very simple Socratic procedure.

Let us examine the stages of thinking regarding the problem of juvenile delinquency. When asked to give his opinion as to its probable cause, a respondent might offer the typical explanation, "It is due to lack of discipline in the home." While this is a sensible answer, it carries the analysis only to the first stage. Not until the respondent is asked to go to the second stage—"Why do you say that? Why is there a lack of discipline, and what bearing does this have on juvenile delinquency?"—is he forced to use his mind and begin to probe into the problem in a more thorough manner. The answer to the questions posed at this second stage might evoke some such answer as, "Parents do not recognize their responsibilities today, and they are too lazy or too indifferent to bother with instructing their children." Or the person being questioned might say that in a home where the parents are undisciplined themselves, it is inevitable that the children will follow their example.

Now we come to the third stage, repeating again the very simple question: "Why do you say that? Why do parents not recognize their responsibilities? Why are they undisciplined themselves?" Trying to answer these, or similar questions, requires even greater mental effort on the part of the person being questioned and takes him to levels that he probably had never reached in his previous thinking.

Of course, the questioning need not stop at this third stage. It can proceed until the respondent is exhausted—or at least until he has no further thoughts on the subject. He may not have come to the right solution (even assuming that there is one), but at least three important benefits will have been reaped: he is certain to have a better comprehension of the problem; he will have been forced to use his higher mental powers; and finally, he will almost certainly be nearer to a correct solution of the problem than he was before he carried it through to the third stage.

This procedure, used with such telling effect by Socrates, has been neglected in the centuries since. Except in special situations, there is no systematic effort made today to teach students to think through a problem—certainly not to the point of carrying their analyses to the third or fourth stages.

If this type of training could be carried on long enough to establish a thinking habit, the effect inevitably would be to raise the quality of thinking of the whole population. Unless it becomes part of the educational program—unless there is a sustained and systematic effort to show how problems can be thought through, and how difficult problems, when carefully analyzed, can usually be reduced to simple problems—the great majority of citizens will never acquire very great facility in this respect.

It should be emphasized that thinking through a problem is quite different from discussing it. Many educators from Dewey's time onward have assumed that they were teaching students to solve problems by the discussion of current issues. Such a course seldom takes the student beyond what has been said in the most recent issues of the daily press. It would be unusual to find students sufficiently prepared to arrive at solutions on the basis of the scattered bits of knowledge they possess and the limited time they can give to an analysis in depth of any issue. The chief virtue of such a course is to interest students in current issues, at least to a point where they will devote more time each week to the front page of their newspapers. It is questionable whether this type of instruction has any real value in teaching students to think through problems and to arrive at new solutions.

Decision Making

Having dealt in part with problem solving, we can now turn to the other side of the coin—decision making. Although problem solving and decision making seem to involve the same mental operations, this is not the case. One requires analysis in depth; the other, a projection of alternate courses of action.

Many books have been written on the subject of decision making since World War II, chiefly to help executives and those who aspire to executive positions. With growing automation in industry and the increased use of data-processing equipment, a whole new field of specialization has been opened to those interested in decision theory and practice.

Some of the developments in the field will be touched upon later. Here we are concerned with the feasibility of training students in decision making as an integral part of their educational program.

The essential process of reaching decisions was described by John Dewey as comprising three steps:

What is the problem?
What are the alternatives?
Which alternative is best?

While these are the bare bones of the process, it can readily be seen that if we can train individuals to increase the number, or improve the quality, of the alternatives to be considered, and if we can train these persons to select the best alternative more often, the process of decision making will improve accordingly. Examination of the decisions that are reached by ordinary persons in the course of their daily lives leads inevitably to the conclusion that much improvement could be made through a training program carried on in the schools as part of a program of training the mind.

Beginning with the third and final step described by Dewey—the selection of the best alternative—the goal becomes one of training students to select the "best" alternative with greater certainty. In the course of weighing the pros and cons of each alternative—a process that in itself can be improved by practice (often by merely making a list with pencil and paper)—a procedure similar to that described earlier under problem solving can be employed to great advantage.

This method consists of projecting the likely consequences of each alternative to additional stages. Students can be trained to carry such projections at least one full stage beyond the point they normally would, in this manner improving substantially their likelihood of choosing the best. In addition to helping them predict more accurately the consequences of their actions, the process requires a great amount of "brain stretching," which of itself must be included as one of the real benefits of such a proposed training program. To think ahead, to project a course of action into the distant future, requires both imagination and a concentration of mental effort that often proves too much for the untrained and the mentally lazy.

The trained thinker, the intelligent person, carries his projections from stage to stage. After he has considered the probable consequence of each alternative, he asks himself, "And *then* what is likely to happen?" To take the second step requires more mental effort. Few persons carry their thinking this far except under pressure. When it comes to taking the third step—projecting one's thinking to the third stage of consequences—even greater imagination and concentration are required. To go on to the fourth, and fifth, stages becomes something of a mental feat. However, the farther one can and does go, the more certain he can be that the best alternative is chosen.

This very simple procedure, as it might be worked out in a school training program and as it relates to the decisions that students themselves typically have to make, can be illustrated by the following example. Henry Smith is a young man of eighteen years, a senior in high school, with grades a little above average. During the next month he must decide what to do about college. His choices, as he sees them, are three:

1. He can enter a small liberal arts college in his state. The college has a good reputation but has no particular distinction.

2. He can enter the state university, a much larger institution, which offers liberal arts and professional courses.

3. He can stay at home and go to work in his uncle's furniture store. His uncle is an elderly man, who has promised to turn the business over to him if he will come in at a small salary and work his way up.

Henry believes that he might like to go into business sometime, but otherwise he has no particular ambition to enter any profession. His parents have moderate means, and if he chooses to go to college, he can do so only if he works in the summer and earns some money doing odd jobs while enrolled in college.

Which of these three alternatives should Henry select, and more to the point, how does he go about making his decision? The first step Henry takes is to figure out what will probably happen to him if he goes to the small college, then in turn to make the same projection in the case of the other two alternatives.

His first concern, in case he continues his education at either college or university, is to weigh his chances of meeting the scholastic requirements. He concludes that he can probably do well enough in his academic work to receive a degree. "Most people with college degrees seem to do well," Henry observes. Then he makes his decision to go to the small college because more of his friends are going there. By the same token he dismisses the alternative of going into his uncle's business, since persons who don't attend college "don't do too well in later life."

Henry has gone about as far in his thinking as many young persons do—and older ones, for that matter. He has not projected the consequences of his choice of alternatives very much beyond the first stage.

The next stage in the process would require him to ask himself: What happens then? Specifically, what happens to him when he receives his degree from the college? If he went to the university and received his degree, what would happen? And if he went into his uncle's furniture store, where would he be in four or five years?

If Henry pursues his thinking to the next stage, he would be compelled to wrestle with many uncertainties, and the going would get much more difficult. He must figure out what is likely to happen when he receives his degree from the small college he has decided to attend. What can he do? Where does he get a job? After pondering this question for some time, and recalling what some of the recent graduates whom he knows are doing, he is somewhat disconcerted. None of them seems to be in a very interesting job; none is making a very large salary.

The more he ponders, the more he compares their status with what he might reasonably expect if he were to enter his uncle's business; and the more he thinks about this, the more attractive it looms. He would be far ahead in money, since he could retain what he had saved for college; he would be a junior executive, with more salary and status than the graduates he knows. If he reaches this stage of projection, his decision will be to enter his uncle's business.

But there is the next stage that he must consider. What will happen to him then? Where will he be when he is fifty years old? Will his college-educated friends have a real advantage over him at that point? Will their status be any higher, their lives any happier? Now

Henry must probe into his goals of life—which he has never thought out before, and which are still pretty hazy in his mind.

He decides that educated persons seem to be better adjusted, hold the highest positions in community affairs, and command the greatest respect. He notes that most of the community leaders have university educations and were trained in one of the professions. Therefore, having gone through the tortuous process of projecting his thinking to the third stage, Henry decides that the choice he made at the first stage of this process—to attend the small college— was not the best alternative, and his choice at the end of the second stage—to go into business with his uncle—was not the best. Instead, the decision reached at the third stage—to go to the state university with professional training in business and finance—is the best alternative of the three.

There is, of course, never complete certainty after all this mental work as to which is truly the best alternative. *But there can be no doubt that Henry has improved his chances of choosing the best by following this process.*

It may be argued that every intelligent person carries his decision making to a third or even fourth stage of projection, and that it is therefore unnecessary to teach young people to follow this practice. While this may be true of the exceptionally able person, the evidence is overwhelming that only a few individuals ever do pursue their thinking to these further stages. The newspapers of the nation offer daily examples of national spokesmen whose thinking on a given issue has not proceeded beyond the first stage.

A systematic training program, built around the problems that confront every person, should be of tremendous help to students— and, later on, to the mass of citizens—in arriving at better decisions, to their own personal benefit and to the benefit of the nation.

Creativity

Many scholars insist that it has been the great philosophers, scientists, religious and political leaders, who have brought civilization to its present level. If this theory is correct, progress in the future will depend upon the emergence of great men of like caliber. The role of society, in this situation, is to prepare the seed ground from which the geniuses of tomorrow will spring.

Whatever truth this theory may have as it relates to the past, it is probable that civilization in the future will move forward on a hundred fronts and that the forward thrust will come from thousands of persons, each making a small but definite contribution. Growing complexity in all departments of life leads to higher degrees of specialization; and at each higher level, more persons become involved and more must be credited with the progress made.

If the latter assumption is sound, a case can be made for training and developing the creative abilities of all students, without limiting this training to the few who may have special creative talents and who may later in life emerge as geniuses. At least, it would seem that progress is far more certain if the attempt is made to train the creative abilities of all rather than to search out the few who seem to have special talents.

A number of studies are now underway to identify the personality traits of highly creative persons. The ultimate purpose of these studies is to find ways to predict which students are most likely to succeed in creative pursuits. Other studies are designed to discover the best environment to foster creativity. Much work has been done with children who have a natural creative bent—a bent that somehow becomes dulled in the educational process.

In the search to discover just what the creative process is, too little attention has been given to a factor that seems to be present in the beginning of most creative efforts—dissatisfaction with the *status quo*. The individual who believes that all is well in his particular field of interest is unlikely ever to have the urge to create anything new or better.

The prime factor in creativity, it can be argued, is "divine discontent." The inventor goes to work because he is convinced he can produce something distinctly better than anything now available. The scientist attempts to develop a new theory or a new approach because he feels that present theories or approaches are false or inadequate. The great religious leader believes it imperative that man turn away from present beliefs and practices. The great writer and the great artist are appalled at the thought of following sheep-like in the steps of their predecessors.

Creativity is likely to begin at the point when someone says, "It's stupid to do this just because everyone else does." Having expressed such an opinion, the person who utters it is forced by the very vacuum he has created to produce an original, or at the very least, an unorthodox, alternative. From this it might be concluded that it is not only necessity that is the mother of invention—perversity also plays its part.

If creativity is to be nurtured in the schools, one lesson to be learned is that heresy should be cultivated and not punished. Students should be encouraged to ask at every turn: "What good is this? Isn't there a better way? How do you know this to be true? Why should I do what everyone else does?" This is not calculated to make the teacher's life any easier, nor the student's marks any higher. But it creates the kind of intellectual ferment that forms the basis of original and creative thinking.

An important reason why young children are likely to be regarded as creative is that custom has not had a chance to condition their thinking. In a very real sense they are fancy-free—limited only by the power of their own imagination. Young children are in the fortunate position of not having to unlearn something or make a conscious effort to rid themselves of orthodox ideas. Any type of learning, and especially that sanctioned by authority, sets mental patterns, which in time can become deep mental ruts. The fertile imaginations of the young can carry them along untried paths and into unexplored regions. This is why those who are interested in the creative process have found research with the young so fruitful.

In a sense, this freedom from orthodoxy may help to explain why researchers have never been able to discover a very high correlation between intelligence and creativity. The person who scores high on intelligence tests is likely to have acquired more knowledge in his years than average students and is therefore all too likely to have patterned his thinking along traditional lines. It cannot be denied that the students who get the highest grades are likely to be those who parrot back faithfully what the professor has taught and what the textbook has printed.

One can only imagine what might have happened to man's history if the children of each generation in Paleolithic times had been taught to ask searching questions about the tools used in hunting and preparing food, and the way of life of early man. Certainly it would not have required a quarter of a million years just to put a better edge on a hand ax.

While the need to question the *status quo* is obvious when we think of the past, there may seem to be no compelling reason to do so today. Yet a thousand years hence, future man may look back upon the present with the same incredulity with which we look back into the distant past. He may wonder how we could be so stupid, so crude, so hidebound, and so satisfied in choosing the wrong paths.

If our goal is to reach the next level of civilization at the earliest time, each generation must be trained to question the *status quo*. In fact, the rate of progress can undoubtedly be measured in terms of discontent with present practices and procedures and resistance to the ever-present temptation to let well enough alone.

Creativity, then, has its roots in unorthodoxy. The creative process begins when some person has the courage to say, "No, I won't do this the usual way," and having committed himself, is forced to make full use of his imaginative powers to sweep his intellectual domain for something different and better.

Training Students to Be Creative

Much of the hesitancy scholars display in dealing with the problem of creativity must be charged to the words used in describing the process. In common parlance, persons arrive at creative ideas by hunches, lightning flashes, sudden insight, pure inspiration, dreams, a bolt from the blue. Such words, and others like them, are calculated to frighten almost any scientist and to lead the scholar into believing that he is dealing with spiritualism, not reality.

These words, which seem to the untutored to be descriptive of the process, can lead to many wrong assumptions. The housewife who knows nothing about nuclear physics will certainly never have a sudden hunch about the way protons behave. The man who knows nothing about physiology is never likely to have a sudden insight into how best to restore a heart valve. The student of literature can hardly be expected to have any great inspiration about the way a new bridge should be anchored.

In short, the hunches, the sudden insights, come typically to those who are immersed in a problem and who are struggling to find their way out. While the end product, the new and creative idea, is arrived at by a kind of extralogical process, the stages that lead up to it are almost always the same, and usually follow this order:

The first stage. The individual involved must be sufficiently informed about the problem to be dissatisfied with the usual solutions or procedures.

The second stage. This dissatisfaction usually generates a desire to find a different and a better answer. The desire itself may be strong or weak, depending largely upon two factors: the urgency of the situation and the degree of emotional involvement. Effort must be extended to find a new answer; and other things being equal, the greater the effort put forth, the greater the likelihood of finding a satisfactory answer.

The third stage. The mind scans the usual alternatives and then proceeds to bring up an array of new alternatives, ranging from what seems to have merit to the wholly impractical. Often, after a lapse of time lasting from seconds to months, during which period the mind either consciously or subconsciously carries on the scanning process, the bright particular solution finally emerges. This sudden appearance, seemingly out of nowhere, often assumes a mystical character. Actually there is nothing very mysterious in the process, at least to those who are familiar with the workings of computers;

TRAINING THE MIND / 69

and it only serves to illustrate once again the incredible range and efficiency of the human mind and the fantastic amount of data that it stores and that can be scanned.

All this brings us again to the question: can students be trained to increase their creative abilities? If the analysis of the creative process, as described here, is substantially correct, then the answer to this question must be Yes. In fact, it is possible to follow much the same procedures as outlined previously. To illustrate, let us return to the example chosen for the procedure involved in decision making.

The class in creative thinking has assembled, and the case history of Henry Smith is up for discussion. It will be recalled that the three alternatives Henry presumably faced were: (1) to attend a small college in his state, (2) to attend the state university, (3) to go into business with his uncle who owns a furniture store.

Since the members of the class have been trained to question customary practices and usual alternatives, one student opens the discussion by saying, "These three alternatives sound pretty dull to me. Why doesn't Henry do something different and join the Peace Corps and ask to be sent to South America?"

The discussion then centers about this alternative and what might happen if Henry made such a decision. The consensus is that joining the Peace Corps might be exciting and would broaden Henry's background, but it would probably not help him much if he decided on a business career.

Adding this new alternative has opened the gates for the wider exercise of the imagination of those present. Another student, stimulated by the discussion, presents this new thought: "Since Henry eventually wants to go into business, probably with his uncle, why doesn't he postpone attending college for a year and go to Denmark, where a lot of modern furniture is manufactured for export, to learn all he can about Danish furniture. In this way he could establish himself as something of an expert on modern furniture."

This suggestion strikes the fancy of many of those present, although the problem of how to carry out the idea baffles them. At this point another student enters the conversation to say, "Obviously it is to the advantage of Denmark and her furniture manufacturers to have persons who can promote the sale of their furniture in the United States. Maybe if Henry wrote the Danish ambassador to ask if he could obtain employment in this field in that country, he could earn enough to pay all his expenses." This proposal intrigues the group, and they conclude that this is another important alternative that Henry should add to his original list of three.

The lively discussion over Danish modern furniture has now aroused the imagination of another member of the class. She states that in her opinion modern furniture is lacking in grace and charm, even though it does seem to be practical and relatively inexpensive. "Couldn't something be done to improve the design of modern furniture?" she asks the class.

The class turns excitedly to a discussion of the kind of furniture that is both attractive and practical, and out of the discussion emerge new thoughts on how changes might be made to overcome the austere appearance of modern furniture. Henry, in fact, says he has a design in mind that might answer some of the criticism; and to illustrate his point, he goes to the blackboard to show what might be done. Henry himself has now added still another alternative to his original list.

The design produced by Henry probably would not win any awards or revolutionize the furniture business. The example is only meant to show that there is little mystery in the process of arriving at new ideas. The process starts with the conviction that the usual is not good enough. At this point the imagination, with a little urging, goes to work to produce a whole assortment of new alternatives— some practical and worthy of further consideration, others so fanciful they can be immediately discarded.

Since a decision must be reached as to which of the many alternatives, new and old, is the best, the decision-making process described earlier is called upon. The probable consequences of each alternative are projected, and the decision as to the best one is made on this basis. By the simple act of stimulating the imagination to produce different alternatives, new doors have been opened, and the students have been given a lesson in how to avoid the commonplace and to start using their creative powers.

If every school child in the nation were given such training over a long enough period to make it a part of his mental approach to every problem, our society would almost certainly move forward at a faster pace. Every child could boast of new and original ideas, and eventually the number of elders who go to their graves without ever having a single new thought in their lives would be small in comparison with the legion who today never manage to escape from the chains of custom. Progress would be certain, and would be far less dependent upon the emergence of great creative geniuses.

Facts That Educational Planning
Must Recognize

Through polling techniques it is possible to observe and assess the state of mankind. Especially is this true if the research embraces the opinions and attitudes of the general public on the important political, social, and economic issues of the day and if it also includes the worries, beliefs, and aspirations of the people. Polling research can cover many other important areas—the reading habits, viewing habits, buying habits, of all segments of the public. The researcher can determine who attends the movies and how often, how many prefer bowling to opera, who visits the art galleries, who buys tickets for symphony concerts.

In research of this type it is standard practice to find out from each person interviewed just how much formal education he has had. In a sense, each person then represents a test of the educational system, since it is possible to relate opinions, knowledge, and behavior to the level of education attained by each person in the cross section. In this manner the product of the educational systems of this and many other nations is being sampled and analyzed continuously in very much the same manner that a manufacturing firm applies sampling techniques to make certain that its products meet quality standards. Regardless of the fact that people do not like to be thought of as sampling units, the procedure of quality control works the same way, whether people or objects are the subject of the test.

The views expressed hereafter are based upon the kind of objective evidence that has proved useful in so many fields. They are based upon an examination of the attitudes and behavior of those who have reached all levels of education, from the first grade to graduate school. The observations are intended to stimulate discussion and to induce readers, particularly educators, to extricate themselves from present controversies long enough to look ahead to the requirements of the future.

Demonstrable weaknesses in the education system will be dealt with first. These include the neglect of writing, the neglect of reading, and the frequent failure to teach students to think quantitatively as well as qualitatively. Opportunities arising from new techniques of instruction will be considered next. Finally, the writer will attempt to outline in a very tentative manner the kind of education he believes will obtain some fifty to a hundred years hence.

The Neglect of Writing

Discussion of the ideal educational program has up to this point placed major emphasis upon the direct training of mental abilities. In addition to this change in educational philosophy, more attention should be directed toward the improvement of the two special skills of writing and reading. The writing of papers, based upon research undertaken by the student, is in itself an effective way to train certain mental faculties.

Writing is neglected today chiefly because the educational program, which is based largely upon classroom instruction, leaves little or no place for it. Teachers are already overburdened, and the task of reading and correcting essays each week cannot easily be fitted into present schedules. If, in addition, a conference were required with each student to discuss his paper, all thought of requiring students to write papers would have to be abandoned.

Clearly, then, the choice must be between the present classroom system and a new kind of individualized education. As between these two alternatives, there can be no doubt that the latter is preferable.

The classroom part of college education is too often a waste of both the students' and the professor's time. Oddly enough, this view is held by many college teachers, but they can do nothing about it because they are locked into a system from which it is all but impossible to escape. Occasional lectures serve a purpose, and in the sciences, laboratory work and classroom demonstrations may be necessary, but the idea that every instructor can profitably occupy nearly an hour of time three times a week for one or two semesters is debatable, to say the least. The same ground can be covered in far less time by appropriate reading outside the classroom.

Nathan Glazer, writing in *Harper's Magazine,* does some plain speaking on this point. A college teacher himself, Glazer says that "a very large part of what students and teachers do in the best colleges and universities is sheer waste. It is not particularly vicious waste, except insofar as it dulls minds and irritates and frustrates students and teachers. Nor does it prevent useful and necessary things from being done in colleges. But it is worth speaking about the waste, not only because it is vast, but because, despite the common awareness that this is so, so little is done about it."

The real sources of this waste, Professor Glazer writes, are the classroom system, the examination system, and the departmental system. Commenting on the faults of the classroom system, he asserts, "Most teachers give lectures that are not as good as the average texts in their fields—which are not very good—and most students have not read enough or heard enough to make the kind of contribution that is worth making in a class of fifty students. But both accept with amazingly little complaint the strait-jacket of the 'course.' "

Many colleges and universities have adopted the seminar system, as Professor Glazer points out. Some are trying to break down the walls that have been erected to separate the various disciplines with a general education curriculum; and a few are trying to do away with grades, substituting, instead, a final comprehensive examination.

The seminar plan does offer some advantages. Through discussion in a small group of from six to twelve, students may be able to clarify their thinking. Participation adds interest. There is a constant temptation, however, for the articulate and the extrovertive students to take the center of the stage when they have little of substance to add to the discussion and only an urge to impress their fellow students or curry favor with the seminar preceptor.

At best, then, the seminar is a compromise. Nevertheless, while it retains many of the faults of the classroom, its merits should not be overlooked. If students learn to express their ideas more cogently, if their ideas are clarified by discussion, these gains must be put down as benefits lacking to a great extent in the class lecture system.

The tutorial system, as used by Oxford, is superior in many ways to the seminar plan. Here the student is on his own, with far less opportunity to "fake it out." He must write an essay every few days, then appear often with three or four of his classmates, before a don or tutor to read his paper aloud for suggestions and criticisms. The paper he has prepared reveals how much thought has been put into its preparation, and how much research. Most important, it brings to light the weaknesses in the student's educational background and thinking processes.

The merits of the tutorial plan of requiring a paper to be written every few days—as opposed to attending class lectures—are clear: The student must do much reading and investigating to find data pertinent to his task. He must exercise his judgment in the selection of material to present. He must organize his facts and his opinions in a logical manner to support the point of view he wishes to establish. And finally, although his views and conclusions may not be entirely original, he must do his own independent thinking.

When a student has produced such a paper, based upon his own research and his own thinking, the learning experience is retained in an extraordinary way. By contrast, the same material obtained from lectures and textbooks is often rapidly forgotten. Add to these merits the benefits that come from gaining facility with the written word, and the over-all advantages of the tutorial system to the individual student loom large indeed.

An attempt to provide some of the benefits of this type of training has been made by the colleges that require a senior thesis and, in some institutions, a junior thesis as well. This requirement has much to recommend it, but again it is still a compromise. The senior and junior thesis project all too often has the great fault of placing too much emphasis on form and not enough on content. The number of footnotes and the length of the bibliography take on great importance. Emphasis is rarely placed upon original thinking; rather, the goal is the attempt to be "scholarly," with ideas and facts cribbed from encyclopedias and other sources. Students acquire skill in what can be described as "interlarding." One sentence is borrowed from one reference book, a second from another, and so on, until something just short of plagiarism emerges. Needless to say, original and independent thinking are sacrificed in the process.

College administrators who have been queried as to why they do not give up the present system for the tutorial plan usually advance the argument of cost. Thirty or forty students in a college classroom can be taught more cheaply, these administrators claim, than one student, or even two or three students, spending one or two hours a week, on the average, with a don or tutor. This may be true, especially in those colleges where there are relatively few teachers in proportion to the number of students; but in those institutions where one teacher is employed for every ten or twelve students, the cost of the tutorial system ought not to be much greater than the present classroom system.

The Neglect of Reading

Bacon's famous aphorism, "Reading maketh a full man, conference a ready man, and writing an exact man," is, if anything, an understatement of the truth. Writing not only makes an exact man; it makes a good thinker. Reading not only fills man with knowledge; it permits him to live many lives—to take part in the great events of history, sit at the feet of philosophers, consort with kings.

Reading is an equalizer. The person who has not been fortunate enough to attend college can, through a planned program of reading, become as well educated as those who win their degrees.

Words are the tools of thought, and vocabularies are built by reading. Abstract thinking is entirely dependent upon language. In fact, all thinking above the very lowest level is based almost entirely upon word concepts. The size of one's vocabulary is closely related to educational achievement, as pointed out earlier.

Reading, it can be seen, plays an extremely important role in the development of higher intellectual capacities. This is the reason Americans should be concerned about the lack of interest in reading displayed by adults of the nation and the lack of attention given to the establishment of lifelong reading habits in the schools.

The number of books sold in America in both hard-cover and pocket-size editions seems impressive. If to this number, sold in bookstores, newsstands, drug stores, and similar places, the number of books lent by the public libraries of the country is added, it seems that America is a country of book readers. Nothing could be farther from the truth. The great number of books bought and borrowed is accounted for by a surprisingly small proportion of the total population. In fact, one adult in five in the population accounts for more than 80 percent of all books bought and read.

In one study—limited to college graduates—it was discovered that one in ten could not name the author of *any* of these twelve books: *An American Tragedy, Babbitt, The Canterbury Tales, Gulliver's Travels, Leaves of Grass, The Old Wives' Tale, Utopia, Vanity Fair, Origin of Species, The Wealth of Nations, Rubaiyat,* and *Tom Jones.* Four in ten could not name more than three. The over-all average for the college graduates tested was only four of the twelve books.

The general lack of interest in books in America is reflected in the number of bookstores. When college bookstores are excluded (they handle mostly textbooks), there are only about two thousand stores that stock a fairly complete line of hard-cover books. In the Scandinavian countries, Great Britain, and France the number of bookstores, in proportion to population, is far greater than it is in the United States.

The reading of magazines and newspapers in America does not account for this difference. In almost all of the other countries mentioned, the number of newspapers read is higher per capita than in the United States, and the circulation of the leading magazines is generally greater when placed on the same population basis. If Americans devoted half the time that they presently give to television to the reading of books, the total number of books read by adults would be increased tenfold.

Why do so many American adults read so few books? The available evidence points to many reasons. The most obvious is that the virtues of reading are seldom extolled or, in American parlance, "sold" to the public. Very few of the parents who plan to send their children to college—and most parents do—appreciate the importance of verbal facility, as acquired by reading, in passing college board examinations. Nor do they realize how difficult it is for the poor or the slow reader to keep his grades high enough to stay in college, once he is admitted.

In many school systems teachers are so overburdened with work that in their own private lives they have less time to read than they should. Possibly the drudgery of the drill work that they are compelled to perform leads them to want to escape from books of all kinds. Be that as it may, there is little evidence that teachers convey to their students any real or lasting enthusiasm for reading.

If teachers must share some of the blame, then parents must assume even more. It is hardly to be expected that a child will develop a great interest in reading if his parents display no enthusiasm for books. If parents spend their leisure hours looking at mysteries and westerns on television, their children will not seek excitement in books. If a family believes that books are unimportant and makes no provision for them in the home, it is likely that the next generation will accept the same point of view. Evidence that this is the case is offered by another dismal statistic. Whereas more than nine out of ten homes in the United States have television sets, only one in every five of the new homes now being built includes any space for books.

Ironically, it is the very plethora of books, the superabundance of titles, which must be put down as another reason for the lack of interest in books. Thomas Jefferson is reputed to have learned a half-dozen languages to enable himself to read all the important books extant. In the present era, with thousands of new books pouring forth yearly from the presses of the world, the task of reading the important books in just one field of interest becomes all but impossible.

A new need, therefore, has arisen, which must be recognized. This is the need to help persons in the selection of books which they will discover to be interesting and rewarding. The avid reader will always find his way about. It is the non-reader and the occasional reader who need help, and since these infrequent readers make up the bulk of the adult population the goal of finding engaging books for them assumes prime importance.

Every time an individual who has not developed a love of books is induced to read a book which he finds to be extremely dull—no matter what its intrinsic merit—the likelihood of converting him into a regular book reader is reduced accordingly. More thought, therefore, must be given to the care and nursing of the potential reader, and every individual who is old enough to read must be placed in this category.

The task of finding the right book for the right person at the right time is formidable, but this must be the goal if we are ever to convert millions of non-readers into readers. Acceptance of this viewpoint—that interest in books, for most persons, must be carefully nurtured—will almost certainly be the first step in correcting many present practices that are demonstrably ineffective.

We must admit that reading interest has often been dulled by well-meaning teachers and librarians, who have insisted that students read the classics before their literary tastes were developed enough to appreciate them. Taste in every department of life must be cultivated over many years. If one is brought up in a non-wine-drinking family, it is not likely that he will appreciate the bouquet of a fine vintage wine. The child whose diet has been limited largely to meat and potatoes will not like ortolans. The same is true of books.

Unfortunately, many college upperclassmen are unable to appreciate the classics. Unless the teacher can impart some of his own enthusiasm for the great books to his students, many will never develop their literary tastes to a point of enjoying these books. If the usual classroom treatment is accorded them, the future will only repeat the past—the great majority of students will ignore them. When gifted teachers are not available, a better policy is to attempt to upgrade the taste of students by planned stages.

In at least one high school, students are urged to write their comments on a card attached to every library book. If they like the book, they can say so in their own patois; if they think the book is terribly dull, they are encouraged to record this opinion. By such a simple device students can choose with greater certainty the books that are suitable to their own tastes and interests. Moreover, because they find the time spent reading such books worth the effort, they are likely to go on liking books, even after they have finished their high school or college careers.

The process of upgrading the public's tastes, whether in books or in other departments of life, has never been accorded much attention. Certainly, no systematic effort has ever been made to achieve this purpose on a national scale. Existing low levels of taste are much discussed and regretted, but as with the weather, the prevailing view is that not much can be done about such things.

When something is attempted, all too often the mistake is made of urging those involved to go too far too fast. Such knowledge and experience as we do possess suggest that the best way to improve taste is to proceed by easy stages.

In the case of books, the upgrading process must start with adequate facts about the taste of each individual and must proceed through the selection of books of better quality that are still within the range of honest appreciation on his part. Progress upward is necessarily slow, but it is also sure. Meanwhile it must not be forgotten that it is better to read books of the lowest order rather than to read no books at all.

The best single index of the cultural level of any community, state, or nation is the number and quality of books read by its adult citizens. When this fact is recognized by Americans, their competitive spirit should lead them to a serious examination of their own reading interests and those of their fellow citizens. From such an examination many fruitful suggestions may emerge for lifting America from its present lowly position. Books must take on some of the importance that they held for Erasmus, who said, "When I get a little money, I buy books; and if any is left, I buy food and clothes."

The Need to Teach Students to Think Quantitatively

A revolution in the teaching of mathematics is now underway in the United States, with the likelihood that within the foreseeable future many students will be able to cope with higher mathematics at an early age, as Maria Montessori once predicted. Children have always had the mental capacity to learn higher mathematics; only custom and the lack of imagination and experimentation have stood in the way.

Students in past years often acquired an unreasonable fear of this subject, with the result that relatively few had the courage to enroll in mathematics courses in high school or college when the decision was left to them. With proper teaching methods, this fear can be dispelled, and studying mathematics can take on all the enjoyment of a game.

The world of the scientist is the world of numbers, and the educated man must learn to think in quantitative terms. Lord Kelvin, the famous British scientist, made this observation: "I often say that when you can measure what you are speaking about and express it in numbers, you know something about it; but when you cannot express it in numbers, your knowledge is of a meager and unsatisfactory kind."

H. G. Wells once predicted that "statistical thinking will one day be as necessary for efficient citizenship as the ability to read and write." That day is already here. Public opinion, which plays so important a role in a democracy, must be interpreted in quantitative as well as qualitative terms if it is to be understood and if it is to have influence.

One of the areas neglected even in present mathematics courses is the study of the laws of probability, which form the basis of all science and impinge upon daily life in countless ways. Whether we play games, make business decisions, invest in the stock market, or interpret survey results, we operate on the basis of our expectations, which in turn rest upon the laws of probability. We bet on a horse, or a football game, or a political candidate, on hunches—which are our own private interpretations of the laws of chance.

These same laws of probability bring within practical reach a whole world of social, economic, and political information. Through sampling procedures and the application of the laws of probability, it is possible to study small samples of the public, or any other statistical universe, and be virtually certain that the part, if carefully selected, will accurately represent the whole. A few thousand persons can, in this manner, represent a million or a hundred million within predictable and small limits of error.

Because of its low cost, the sampling method brings into being a whole new world of useful data. Governments can quickly and accurately determine the number of persons who are unemployed, who are ill, who are informed or uninformed about government policy, who own their own homes, who have television sets, or any other of a thousand kinds of information that may be important. Business concerns can likewise answer many of their problems that have to do with consumer preference and use of particular products. The media of mass communication can estimate how many persons they are reaching, what programs or editorial features are most popular, what advertisements and commercials are most effective. These are only a few of the many facts that can be gathered quickly and inexpensively by the use of modern sampling methods and the laws of probability.

The uses of survey data are so many that all students should have at least some knowledge of the procedures involved and the problems and pitfalls encountered. Since the methods are easy to understand and the laws of probability easy to demonstrate, this study might well be included in the secondary school curriculum.

The world of the scientist is a world not only of numbers but of larger and larger numbers. In the process of learning to think in quantitative terms, therefore, we must learn to think in those quantities with which science must increasingly deal. Even in his daily, nonscientific life the ordinary citizen has to cope with figures that he may be able to read but unable to comprehend. Ask your neighbor how much America's national debt is, and you will note that he is likely to confuse millions and billions. Ask him to tell you the population of China, Russia, India, or Australia, and he will reveal his unfamiliarity with the world of large figures. Ask him to translate an appropriation of fifty billion dollars for defense into the tax required from a typical American family, and even though he may have had courses in mathematics, he is likely to get his naughts confused.

In ancient times astronomers were able to identify only a few thousand stars with the naked eye. When telescopes were devised, the number of stars increased to a million. Largely because of the work of Harlow Shapley, we now have some conception of the number of stars in our own galaxy—a number that reaches the staggering total of one hundred billion! The almost unimaginable distances with which astronomers must deal has meant that even the system of using naughts has been found impractical. They have therefore come to use a unit called the parsec. Even the use of the parsec, however, has had to be modified in the light of new findings. The kiloparsec and the megaparsec have had to be introduced. The distance of the galaxy nearest our own is estimated at one megaparsec, or 1,000,000 parsecs, a parsec being the distance that light travels (at the rate of 186,000 miles a second) during the course of 3.26 years.

At the other extreme in size and distance new units of measurement must be found to express minuteness. The biologist uses the "micron," usually called the mu, and the mu is only one thousandth of one millimeter, or one twenty-five-thousandths of an inch!

These are new ways to express the dimensions of the universe in which we live—ways that the students of tomorrow must comprehend. The electronic computer helps make our knowledge of this universe more manageable, but its use places even greater importance upon learning our way about in the world of big numbers.

The Case History Approach

Until students actually begin their professional or technical training, the educational program might well be described as the Period of Great Confusion. High school students have been asked in many surveys what they believe to be the greatest benefits they are deriving from their education. Most answer in terms of such rationalizations as, "I am finding new friends," "It is helping me build my character," "It is improving my personality." In fact, their answers differ little from what might be expected if they were spending their days at dancing school.

Amazingly few think of the benefits of their education in terms of the accepted goals of education. Very few students indicate that they are learning how to think, that they are developing an interest in acquiring knowledge, that they are better able to understand the problems of the nation or the world, or that they are acquiring a broad cultural background that will enhance their enjoyment of life.

Americans are, of course, a practical people, and it is not unexpected that their children want to know, "What good is this?" "Why should I devote time and effort to this subject?" Since they find it difficult to relate subject matter to their own lives, and since few teachers take the trouble to enlighten them on this point, it is inevitable that they approach their studies with something short of enthusiasm.

It could be argued that it makes little difference whether they like or dislike their schoolwork just so long as they do it. However, the natural consequence of accepting the view that education is a bitter pill is that, after high school or college, it leads those who are no longer compelled to swallow this pill, to shun and abhor it.

The vital spark in the whole learning process is interest. Unless it can be kept alive and glowing through the years of formal education and into the adult years, education has largely failed in its primary purpose. The great question, to which far too little attention has been addressed by the educators, is how to keep this feeble spark alive.

One answer is the case history method. Personal involvement is one of the secrets of interest. In dealing with real persons in real-life situations, the student becomes involved; he identifies himself easily in such situations. His intellectual curiosity impels him to stay with the problem until he has worked out a solution, or at least until he knows how it should come out.

The case history method has gained great popularity in graduate schools of business as an effective teaching method. Why its merits have been overlooked for instructing students at all levels, from elementary school to graduate school, is something of a mystery, particularly since historically it is probably the oldest method. The myth and the parable are essentially case histories, and their influence upon mankind is incalculable.

The case history method offers perhaps the best method that mankind has yet found to transmit wisdom as opposed to knowledge. Each new generation stands on the shoulders of the last in respect to knowledge; but wisdom is more than knowledge—it is the distillation of man's whole experience.

While this experience, and the wisdom that grows out of it, is all but impossible to hand down from generation to generation (we would be thousands of years advanced in the art of living if it could), the case history method provides at least an imitation of, or a substitute for, experience. We can learn vicariously from the experience of others, especially when that experience is conveyed in an easy-to-follow and realistic manner.

One of the tragedies of man is that the experience of the millions and millions of human beings who have inhabited the earth goes almost entirely unheeded and unused. Each generation, like the lemmings, repeats the same errors and suffers the same fate.

While the stock of knowledge constantly grows, the ability of man to manage his own life, to master the art of living, has advanced little since earliest times. The wisdom of one era of history is often lost, or more often ignored, by those who chance to be born in later times.

If a way could be found to transmit wisdom, then each generation would live happier and more satisfying lives than the generation that preceded it. In this fashion mankind would improve markedly in the art of living as time goes on.

Instruction, exhortation, preachments, whether by teacher, parent, or cleric, have proved of little value in transmitting wisdom. Only experience can do this—or its best substitute. In earlier epochs this was the parable, the fable, and the myth. And the nearest modern equivalent of these is the case history, the educational value of which has never been fully recognized.

Programmed Instruction

Since the time of Socrates the proper role of the teacher has been debated. Should he guide or should he drill? Should the teacher lead the student to use his own mind or should he tell the student what to think? Is learning an exciting adventure in which both teacher and pupil share, or is it a matter of listening to lectures, reading condensations of knowledge in thick textbooks, regurgitating this information in daily quizzes, and then forgetting the whole dreary business as soon as convenient?

The appearance of teaching machines, or what might be described more aptly as self-instruction machines, comes at a fortuitous time. The machine itself is just another mechanical gadget and is not even essential in many learning situations. What is important is the programmed material, which can be presented to the student either with or without benefit of machine.

The task of creating programmed material represents an intellectual feat of the first order. Anyone who attempts to organize educational material in an orderly and logical manner, simple enough for the slowest student to follow, will discover that he must have an intimate knowledge of the subject and also great insight into the teaching process. In fact, the developing art of programming may shed much light on the best instructional methods.

Only after long and careful experimentation is a program likely to emerge that is demonstrably better than the usual type of instruction students receive in a given subject. The burden of proof must always be on the program. Unless it can be proved to be superior to oral instruction, it obviously has little justification in the school.

In those areas of learning where drill work is important, machines are likely to prove better than teachers—at least when time and patience are factors. The machine is adapted to the rate of learning of each child. He proceeds from one lesson to the next only when he has mastered each step. Since teaching machines lend to the learning process some of the character of a game, they can add interest to rote learning. And they do have one very great and undeniable advantage—machines permit the learning to go on outside of school hours, without a teacher in attendance.

Students, henceforth, can go as far and as fast as they choose in many areas. Self-education, for the first time, begins to have a real meaning and a real place in the educational program.

Most important, the program method can perform a tremendous service for American education by freeing teachers to assume the role they always should have filled—that of guide and leader and not mere drill master. Machines in the educational world can perform the same service that machines do in business and industry. They can relieve the teacher of tiresome and repetitive tasks, leaving him free to devote his energies to more interesting and higher pursuits. Almost certainly they will find a place at the highest levels of education as well as the lowest.

With the spread of this type of instruction, new importance will be placed upon the teacher's ability to inspire and to lead, with the result that the teacher's influence will be felt to a far greater extent in the life of the student. With this new influence, teachers will be accorded the greater respect they richly merit.

Expansion of Knowledge and Reading Speed

Many writers have pointed out that more new knowledge has been created during the last three decades than in the entire period of recorded history. If this vast expansion of factual data is properly described as an explosion, perhaps a new word will have to be coined to describe what the future has in store.

The volume of research will almost certainly continue to grow at an increasing rate to meet the demands of industry, government, and the many professions. The enrollments in graduate colleges continue to increase, which means that an ever increasing number of professionally trained researchers will be prepared to undertake new research.

From America and Europe a constantly increasing flow of new facts and findings is likely. Moreover, looking ahead a few years, we can see the other nations of the world beginning to swell the stream of knowledge as their educational levels are increased and as interest turns more and more to research.

The people of the world, therefore, must prepare for an inundation of new knowledge and take measures to deal with it intelligently. The great increase in the stock of information in many fields poses specific problems. Students will be forced to spend more time in college, preparing for their careers, or cover more ground before they reach college. Special efforts will have to be taken to separate the important from the unimportant, to prune textbooks, which all too often are filled with trivia, and to discard other material that, while good, is not worth the time required to peruse it.

One development that has made its appearance at a fortunate moment is the search for new ways to increase reading speed. Many promising experiments are underway, with the likelihood that methods will be devised to enable the typical person to double or treble his reading speed.

One of the more intriguing methods has been advanced by Mrs. Evelyn Nielson Wood, whose organization is known as Reading Dynamics Institute. Her interest in this field is reported to have begun when she served as a counselor in the Salt Lake City high schools. It was there that she reached the conclusion that the root of most students' problems was slow reading.

Mrs. Wood set out to learn from those persons who could read and comprehend words at remarkable speeds. After investigating the reading techniques of this group, she studied the reading methods of ordinary persons, who read at speeds ranging from 150 to 200 words per minute.

Close observation of the practices followed by the fast readers, contrasted with those followed by the slow readers, enabled her to evolve her own technique. Basically, her method involves reading rapidly down the page, rather than across, and allowing the eyes to trigger the mind directly by eliminating the middle step of saying, hearing, or thinking the sound of words.

Apart from Mrs. Wood's success in demonstrating that reading speeds can be greatly increased, her experience suggests that the brain of man is able to absorb material at a far faster rate than anyone has imagined. Once this truth is accepted, the door will be opened for many experiments. In time, the method developed by Mrs. Wood, or similar ones, will gain acceptance in the schools and become the regular reading practice of the public. With an increase in reading speed, man has one way to cope with the ever-rising flow of knowledge.

The Educational Program Envisaged

To be realistic about education in the United States, one must take account of the extraordinary resistance to change in this field. Dr. James Allen, Commissioner of Education of New York State, has said that as much as fifty years elapse before an invention or innovation in education is put into widespread practice. Cultural lag is unduly long in all fields, but in education it far exceeds that found in most industries, and in such fields as medicine and agriculture.

The importance of education is evidenced in many ways: by the vast number of persons directly involved, by the vast expenditures of public money required, and by the tremendous effect it has on the life of the nation. Yet, as Dr. John M. Stainmaker, president of the National Merit Scholarship Corporation, has pointed out, "No activity involving so many people and so much money has done so little to find out about itself; the nature of its raw material, the effectiveness of its processing and the quality of the finished product."

In a sense, it is this very lack of concern with improvement and lack of intelligent, imaginative planning that presents an opportunity for great progress in the future. So little has been done to help students actualize their potentialities—to develop their intellectual capabilities—that almost any planned effort in this direction is likely to bring amazing results.

Guidelines are needed to point the way, although the time has not yet come to spell out detailed programs. After looking honestly at the present shortcomings of the educational system, and taking account of what is being discovered about the capacities of the human brain, we can then be in a good position to direct the kind of research that should precede any far-reaching changes. With this thought in mind, some general views can be offered that may be useful in planning the educational program for the future.

In the educational process, far greater responsibility should be assumed by the individual as opposed to the school. The years of formal education should be regarded as only one part of a lifetime plan. The learning process is essentially one of self-education, and this viewpoint must be deeply imbedded in the thinking of both educators and citizens. The years following graduation from high school, or college, therefore, need to be planned with the same care as the years in school.

Major emphasis during the first ten years of schooling should be placed upon the direct training of mental abilities, to teach students to make optimum use of their minds in their adult life, as well as to enable them to accomplish far more during their years in school. Training the mind directly, not leaving its development to chance, offers the greatest hope of lifting man to a higher level of civilization and, for this very reason, represents the educator's greatest challenge.

With the rapid expansion of knowledge, the need grows to train citizens of the future to separate the important from the unimportant. Minds must be trained to cope with facts, not merely to store them.

The teacher ought to play a different role. Instead of serving as a drill master, forcing education upon students whose intellectual curiosity has long since been killed by a system that removes the excitement and most of the reality from the process of learning, the teacher should be able to assume the more important role of guide and counselor. The dull and repetitious part of the teacher's present work can be performed by programmed teaching, or self-instruction machines.

By better planning and the elimination of much that is of minor and doubtful importance, it should be possible not only to carry out the educational program outlined in the preceding pages, but to include, in the present four-year high-school period, most subjects that are now taught to college undergraduates. The duplication in high school and college education is already great, and most college courses could easily be absorbed by students of high school age if they had the right preparation.

The proposals that follow as to the proper time to include certain training and subjects in the educational program are to be regarded only as suggestions. Experience, and experiments, must be relied upon to answer the question as to the best time to introduce each type of training and each subject. With this qualification, the following specific proposals can be set down.

The elementary years, or roughly that period from five to thirteen years of age, should be devoted largely to the direct training of mental abilities, particularly the training of perception, concentration, and organization, and to the teaching of basic skills. During this period elementary school children should be taught to read rapidly by the newest methods and should be introduced to mathematics. A practical, speaking familiarity with one or two foreign languages should also be part of the curriculum.

During the high school years the direct training of mental abilities should be continued, with particular attention directed toward problem solving, decision making, and creative thinking. Extensive reading should be required in the humanities, thereby covering most subjects now taught in college. In their last two years of high school, students could be required to write papers based upon their reading and research, with classroom time reduced accordingly. In general, the secondary schools should cover most of the liberal arts subjects now reserved for college.

The colleges and universities would become graduate schools in this plan. The classroom-lecture system might well be abandoned in favor of the tutorial system. The course, or departmental system, should also be abolished. The educational center of the university should be the library. Students ought to be permitted to cover the areas of learning of interest to them and at a rate of speed best fitted to their needs and capacities. Degrees could be awarded on the basis of a comprehensive examination similar to that given today for advanced degrees.

If the ultimate goal of education is to enable man to realize his maximum potential, then certainly a new educational philosophy is required. The broad outlines of an educational program to fit this new philosophy have been sketched in the preceding pages. The program is designed to train students to develop their ability to solve problems, to make decisions, to organize and plan their work, to be more creative, and to be independent in their point of view. The program, it is hoped, will arouse the intellectual curiosity of students and help them retain the excitement of learning, not only through the years of formal schooling but throughout adult life. It is designed to give every high-school graduate the present equivalent of a college education, covering in twelve years what now requires sixteen. College education, in turn, will become graduate school education.

As outlined, the program is designed to take greater advantage of the experience of man—his wisdom as opposed to his knowledge— with the goal of helping students live a happier and more useful life. Finally, it is designed to give each student a custom-tailored education, as far as is practicable, in place of the present mass education.

PART III

THE POTENTIALITIES
OF COLLECTIVE EFFORT

The Opportunities

The preceding chapters of this book have dealt with the great opportunities inherent in the largely unused mental capacities of the individual. This part will deal with the equally great opportunities that are possible through collective effort. Up to this point in history, society has failed to make effective use of the talents of the great mass of people. It is a truism to say that the greatest untapped resource of mankind is brain power.

Strangely, throughout history, no systematic effort has been made to use this great and awesome force in the service of mankind. On the other hand, perhaps this situation is not so strange. For hundreds of thousands of years man's inventive genius has been directed almost exclusively toward the making of better tools and instruments. The various stages in the progress of man are, in fact, marked by his increasing skill in tool-making.

Except for brief moments in history, man has not turned his inventive talents to the forging of new and better political and social instruments. The production of better tools, goods, and services has been his daily concern. The remarkable progess that is possible in the discovery of new and better ways to deal with social ills has never gripped his imagination or galvanized his energies.

Eons from now we may look back upon the present era as a time when this great resource of man—his brain power—was almost entirely wasted. During his earliest existence the problem of keeping alive necessarily occupied most of man's thoughts. However, having freed himself to a great extent from almost complete absorption with physical needs, he can now turn his mind to cultural needs and the solution of problems created by modern civilization.

In these pages an effort will be made to show how the talents of ordinary citizens can be, and should be, utilized to a much greater extent. It will be pointed out that many of our present ways of dealing with the political and military problems of government are demonstrably ineffective; they never will achieve a high level of success because they violate well-established principles of human behavior.

What has never been fully understood is that a new type of collective action is required to move society forward on many fronts. It is not enough to put thousands and thousands of people to work nibbling away at the far edges of our great problems—a constant temptation for all governments. Not only is a special type of collective action necessary, but it must be employed under conditions that maximize the opportunity for applying brain power and minimize the chance for individual prejudice and self-interest to interfere.

Fortunately, enough experience has now been accumulated to enable us to define the operating principles that should be followed in dealing with these problems.

Unsolved Problems and Unused Talents

Dictatorships have a natural advantage over democracies, at least to the extent that they can demand that citizens with special abilities be assigned to the tasks where their talents are most needed. Democracies can require these same services only in time of war, or when war threatens. The weakness of democracy, however, is not this lack of authority over the lives of its citizens; it is the failure to invent effective systems of voluntary service.

The study reported here shows that millions of educated and talented persons in the United States are ready to contribute their time and effort to the solution of political and social problems that beset their communities today; but their services are rarely solicited, simply because no one has bothered to work out a plan for selecting them, no machinery has been devised for using the services of those selected, and no way has been found to make practical use of the conclusions they reach. What is needed, therefore, is the creation, through man's inventive genius, of social and political instruments that can make full use of the vast reservoir of mental power.

In dealing with this and similar situations, an all-important point, usually disregarded, should always be kept in mind: *Political and social instruments must be designed to fit people; it is futile to attempt to change people to fit the instruments.* Stated in another way, it is easier to change forms and institutions than it is to change people. Trying to change people is almost certain to end in failure, which is the chief reason why so many of our present institutions and practices are unsuccessful and need overhauling.

City officials sometimes complain that citizens fail to attend meetings to express their opinions and offer suggestions. However, the very fact that so few of the citizens of a community attend such meetings or volunteer their services—except in those cities where special efforts are made to see that they do—constitutes ample proof that something is basically wrong with the present structure of local government. The people are not to be blamed for their lack of interest; the fault can be attributed to the failure to devise ways of making voluntary service attractive. Apathy will vanish when ways are found to put citizens to work in useful and meaningful ways.

America's Local Problems

How much talent is available to deal with the problems of local communities, and what are the problems, as the public sees them? To answer these questions, a national study was undertaken with the following specific goals in mind: first, to determine which of the many needs and problems are common to the greatest number of towns and cities of the nation; second, to see how much talent is available to work on the solutions of these problems; and third, to suggest ways to utilize the available talent in solving these problems.

Most communities of the nation have their own special problems. At the same time, there are many problems common to communities of all sizes, ranging from the largest to the smallest. In the effort to discover which are the most frequently met problems or needs, the people themselves were consulted. The problems, therefore, are those perceived by the citizens of these communities.

The cross section, or sample, in this survey was constructed so as to represent in correct proportion all areas of the country and all communities of all sizes. The persons interviewed came from all walks of life. The poor man living in a crowded tenement district of a big city had the same opportunity to give his ideas of the problems and needs of his city as the banker living in an exclusive residential district of a suburban community.

Both authorities on local government and ordinary citizens were asked to list all the local problems that seemed important to them. From preliminary surveys the list, which originally contained more than a hundred problems and needs, was finally reduced to thirty-nine.

Ideally such a study should be undertaken in every local community of the nation, but the expense would be enormous and the task of tabulating and reporting the results, overwhelming. By scientific sampling methods the same, or virtually the same, results can be obtained, as pointed out previously.

From the printed list of thirty-nine problems, each person included in the sample chose all the problems that seemed to him to apply to his own community. After the person being interviewed had been given full opportunity to go over the list, he was asked if there were any other problems that came to his mind that were not included on the list. If there were, these problems were recorded by the interviewer.

The list, which by no means exhausts all the local problems in America at this time, does reflect those common to the greatest number of communities, large and small. The order of importance, as shown by the frequency of mention, reveals much about the philosophy of the American people and the trend of their thinking about current issues.

Below, listed in order of frequency of mention, are America's greatest local problems, as the people see them:

1. Property taxes are too high.
2. Not enough attention is being given to juvenile delinquency.
3. There are not enough recreation places for youngsters.
4. The streets and roads are badly in need of repair.
5. The schools are too crowded.
6. The community does not have enough industry.
7. Not enough thought or care is being given to older citizens.
8. There is too much unemployment locally.
9. Children are not required to do enough work at home or at school.
10. The community does not have enough parking areas and facilities for cars.

11. The best people in the community are not active in local government.

12. A slum clearance program is needed.

13. The community has poor public transportation.

14. There is too much (cheap) politics in local government.

15. More effort should be devoted to beautifying the community by such means as planting flowers, painting buildings, and cleaning up.

16. Traffic congestion.

17. Not enough housing has been provided for older people.

18. There is need for more public housing.

19. The community does not have enough doctors.

20. The community does not have enough hospital facilities.

21. There are not enough cultural interests or activities.

22. The quality of education in the local schools is poor.

23. There is too much racial prejudice.

24. The newspapers are too one-sided in their editorial views.

25. The business center of the city is run down.

26. The courts are too slow to act.

27. The community provides poor police protection.

28. The community has poor sewage disposal.

29. Too much religious prejudice is found in the community.

30. The courts are not equally fair to all.

31. There is too much smoke and dust (smog).

32. The community does not have enough public libraries.

33. There are too many cheap housing developments.

34. There is no civic pride.

35. The community has poor jails or prisons.

36. The community does not have proper fire inspection and protection.

37. There is need to preserve historic places and landmarks.

38. A shortage of water.

39. The community is too industrialized.

As might be expected, the findings reveal wide variations from one section of the country to another and equally wide differences between the large cities and the small towns. At the same time, certain problems seem to be universal. Everywhere in America there is concern about young people. Juvenile delinquency is cited as one of the most important problems, not only in the large cities but in communities of all sizes down to the smallest. Possible solutions of this problem are likewise placed high on the list. The public believes there should be more recreation places for youngsters and that children should be required to do more work at home and at school. Delinquency, in short, is to a great extent a function of idleness, in their opinion.

That most Americans are not too much concerned about improving the cultural advantages of their communities is likewise evidenced by the relatively low position they assign to new libraries, preserving the historic places and landmarks, beautifying the community, and the over-all lack of cultural interests and activities.

The Talent Available

Having surveyed the needs and problems of local communities in the United States, an effort was next made to discover how many persons would be willing to serve on committees dealing with these problems and how much time they would be willing to devote to the work each week.

It is customary for leaders in civic life to bewail the apathy of ordinary citizens. Is the public unwilling to participate in civic affairs, or should the blame be charged to the failure of government to find ways by which ordinary citizens can be encouraged to devote their time and effort to local problems?

The study answers this question definitively. The public is willing to respond, and in numbers that are amazing. When the survey figures are translated into population figures, the results show that millions upon millions of American citizens say they are ready to go to work to help solve the problems that they believe to be important. An astounding amount of talent is available if ways can be found to make use of it.

If the public is so willing to go to work, some public officials may argue, why has there not been greater evidence of this interest? There are a number of answers to this question. Too often, when the public is called in, the purpose is not to help solve problems, but to pass judgment on solutions already reached by the politicians. Many officials regard it as a sign of weakness if they consult the public in areas that they regard as their own responsibility. Others fear that the mere act of bringing in the public might jeopardize political alignments and their own power structures. The idea of massive citizen participation is something new in local government. It has been tried in only a few communities—and, it might be added, with notable success.

For this part of the survey, a representative sample of citizens twenty-one years of age and older was again interviewed from coast to coast. They were carefully selected to comprise an accurate cross section of the entire adult population. Moreover, since in surveys of this type many facts dealing with the socio-economic status of each person interviewed are obtained, it is possible to report the findings by education, age, sex, religion, city size, area of the country, and many other ways.

The questions put to each person were designed to find out if he would be willing to serve on a committee dealing with some local problem, such as housing, recreation, traffic, health, and the like, and if so, how much time he would be willing to give each week for work on such a committee.

Of all persons interviewed, more than six in ten (61.3 percent) said they would be willing to serve on such a committee. Slightly more men than women said they would accept such an invitation; younger adults were found to be slightly more willing than those over fifty. Most important, however, the best educated were found to be most eager to serve. Nearly three out of every four of those who had attended college said they would like to perform such a service for their local communities.

When those who said they would like to serve on such a committee were asked how much time they could give, the number of hours per week averaged slightly more than four hours. Nearly a third of all persons questioned said they would devote more than six hours a week to such work.

When these percentages are translated into national totals, the numbers reach staggering totals. If we assume a total adult population of 100,000,000, the number of persons who say they would take part in the solution of these local problems adds up to 61,300,000.

And if the hours that they say they would be willing to spend each week is calculated, the result reaches the total of 245,200,000 hours per week!

A typical city with a population of 50,000 could likely count upon the efforts of some 20,000 persons. Assuming that each person could give four hours a week to local affairs, the total would be 80,000 hours per week. Or by the same arithmetic, a city of 500,000 could count on approximately 800,000 hours of effort per week from its adult citizens.

These figures represent potentials. Any realist should be quick to recognize that we are dealing here with an idealized situation, with intentions and not behavior. But granting this, and taking full account of every reservation that can be advanced, there still remains an enormous army of citizens who would like to be called upon to perform some public service and who would be willing to devote a surprising amount of time each week to this end.

The question, then, is how to harness the energies and talents of this multitude in the solution of the many problems that confront local communities in all areas of the country. One obvious way is to encourage mayors and other local officials to appoint citizen committees to deal with local problems—appointing as many committees as there are important needs and problems.

The committee approach, as will be pointed out later, has a spotty record of success. However, it must be asserted that the reason for this is probably the way the committee is set up. Many requirements must be met if a committee is to accomplish anything worthwhile. These will be discussed at some length later in this book. Here it may suffice to point out the minimum essentials for success: (1) the problem must be important; (2) persons who comprise the committee must have a particular interest in the problem; (3) members of the committee must represent the major groups in the community; (4) there must be an honest intent on the part of local authorities to make use of the committee's findings; (5) there must be full publicity for the committee's conclusions; and (6) the findings should embrace an action program.

Although committees with a small membership are often regarded as more efficient than large ones, this again is a matter of skill in organization. A large committee permits more citizens to become involved—a good thing in itself. Moreover, a large committee permits a wide representation of the many groups found in any community; it also increases the chances of finding persons with imaginative ideas. Lastly, a large committee, representative of the whole community, increases the likelihood that the conclusions of the committee will be accepted and acted upon.

A review of the successful efforts that have been made in various cities during the last decade to meet the many problems with which cities are faced almost always reveals that citizen activity, on a broad scale, is the magic ingredient for producing outstanding achievements. Twelve years of service as the chairman of the jury that selects each year the All-America cities—a program sponsored by the National Municipal League and *Look* magazine—has given the writer an opportunity to study the forces at work in those cities that have sought this honor and have won the All-America awards.

What is true at the local level applies with equal force at the state level. Governor's committees, made up of hundreds of citizens selected from a given state, could be put to work on state problems, with every likelihood that great things would happen as a result of their efforts properly directed.

The question, then, of citizen apathy must be examined from a new point of view. Civic indifference must be charged to the failure of political leaders and social inventors to devise ways to make use of massive citizen effort in a meaningful manner. When such ways are found, citizens will become active, and a tremendous force for community betterment will become readily available.

Experiments in Government

The goals of a democratic society change little, except over long periods of time; but the methods adopted for achieving these goals must be altered as new conditions arise. This is the reason why practices, forms, and systems—the machinery of government—must be scrutinized continuously and why change is so vital to the health of democracy.

Experiments are necessary for progress, even though it is inevitable that some will end in failure. The trial-and-error approach is just as important in government as it is in science. Where there is no experimentation, there is likely to be little progress.

In the following pages, two of many experiments undertaken during the present century will be discussed in some detail. One of these was eminently successful; the other failed to live up to expectations, leaving the problem with which it was concerned still unsolved.

By the turn of the century some political scientists had come to the conclusion that local government was one of the many bad features of American political life. No less an authority than James Bryce held the view that "the government of the cities is the one conspicuous failure of American democracy."

The mayor-council form was the prevailing type of local government in the United States prior to 1903—a form that is still followed in many of America's cities today. In some large cities and in many smaller ones it has proved satisfactory, but as a form of local government it has usually proved inefficient and all too often has opened the door to corruption.

City governments can be so impervious to public opinion, so deeply entrenched in spoils and favoritism, that intelligent and responsible citizens give up in disgust when they try to bring about improvements. "You can't fight City Hall" is a cry of the disillusioned still to be heard in many of America's great cities.

It is this situation that has encouraged the adoption of the council-manager plan by more than half of all cities of the country with populations above 10,000 and by a substantial number of cities of smaller size. The council-manager plan vests all the powers of the city in a council, which is usually elected at large and in nonpartisan elections. The council employs a city manager in much the same way as a school board selects a superintendent. The manager can be removed from office at any time and for any reason. His job is largely administrative: he appoints and directs the department heads, prepares the annual budget, and attends to the business of running the city efficiently. Department heads can be brought in from outside the city if the positions cannot be filled by competent local persons.

The office of city manager first appeared in Staunton, Virginia, in 1908; but it was Sumter, South Carolina, that put the manager under a single elective board in 1913. In the years since then, the council-manager plan has been adopted by a constantly growing list of cities, counties, and towns. The total, as of January 1, 1963, was 1,891 cities and counties, including 57 in Canada. Within another few decades most of the larger cities of the country will have this form of local government.

The council-manager plan corrects a very real shortcoming found at all levels of government. It separates policy-making from administration. It recognizes that these two functions require different talents—in the first instance, to set legislative goals in keeping with public needs, and in the second instance, to operate the government in the most efficient manner. This latter function, it should be emphasized, has little or nothing to do with political ideologies. There is no Republican way to clean the streets of a city, to prevent crime, and to provide fire protection, as opposed to a Democratic way to perform these services. There is only an efficient as opposed to an inefficient way.

Persons who are trained to get work done quickly and inexpensively should be in charge of operations. Such duties should not be shouldered by amateurs or by those who have no liking for this kind of work, and certainly these responsibilities should not be turned over to political hacks who are lacking both in administrative ability and in leadership qualities.

Those who defend the mayor-council system usually advance the argument that, with all of its deficiencies, it is important to the two-party system of the nation. (Actually most of the large cities of this type are nonpartisan.) It is true that local political machines can perform two necessary chores for national parties: they can raise money, and they can get out the vote of party followers on election day. While these are obviously important to the national parties, it should not be forgotten that it is the boss-ridden political machines of our cities that are chiefly responsible for the low opinion of politics and politicians held by most Americans. The necessity to associate with and to play ball with second-rate and often corrupt local politicians has constituted perhaps the chief deterrent to active participation in government by leading citizens.

The council-manager plan removes most of the opportunities for graft. In addition, since members elected to the council do not have to spend their time dealing with the minutiae of the day-to-day operating problems, but only with the policy aspects of these problems, men of higher caliber can be induced to run for council positions.

Americans are not alone in their concern regarding the quality of local government. England, which still clings to its own type of mayor-council system, has also discovered that, for reasons entirely different from those that obtain in the United States, "the most enterprising and the ablest people of the town or district are not attracted to local government." This was the conclusion reached by John Stuart Mill at about the same time that it was becoming apparent in the United States that the system of local government had many faults. Mill wrote, "The greatest imperfection of popular local institutions, and the chief cause of the failure which so often attends them, is the low caliber of the men by whom they are almost always carried on."

Bryan Keith-Lucas of Oxford University, an authority on local government, notes that in England the local councils have the power to appoint on their committees people who are not members of the council, but they fail to use this power except in instances required by law. The effect, he believes, is to keep local administration in the hands of a narrow group and to overlook the many able and willing people who have knowledge and experience to make valuable contributions. To keep local government in England from stagnating and to enable it to adapt itself to the new problems confronting local government in the modern world, Keith-Lucas urges that local authorities be given the power to experiment and, if need be, to alter electoral methods, abolishing those systems and forms that now seem to serve no useful purpose.

Ironically, America imported the mayor-council system from England; in return we have exported the council-manager plan. Indeed, many Canadian cities have already adopted this form of local government, as have all of the twenty-six counties of Eire and three of its four largest cities.

The city manager plan is an experiment that succeeded, but it should be stressed that this plan has achieved its greatest success in dealing with administrative problems. There is still the need to invent new ways to attract the very ablest citizens to office, to make full use of the talents of the people, and to encourage much greater citizen participation in the affairs of the city.

An Experiment That Failed to
Live Up to Expectations

Not all attempts to correct the shortcomings of democratic procedures end in success. One experiment that started with great promise has not lived up to expectations, even though it has brought about an improvement in the moral climate of politics.

Just before the turn of the century, the American public became alarmed at the extent to which corrupt political bosses and machines had gained power and were dictating the choice of candidates for all public offices. The party convention, which was the usual method of selecting candidates before this period, could easily be packed with party henchmen, who were there to do the bidding of the machine.

A reform wave to curb this power struck the nation, and out of it came a plan for a direct primary that would offer rank-and-file members of a political party the chance to put up a candidate in opposition to the one chosen by the machine. With the existence of such a threat, it was believed that the machine would have to put up better men for office.

Robert M. LaFollette, the nation's leading advocate of the direct primary, induced his home state of Wisconsin to enact the first statewide direct primary in the year 1903, when he was governor. Within a few years all but four states had enacted compulsory direct primary laws.

Corrupt political machines, which exist on patronage and the spoils of office, are less common and less brazen today than they were in 1900, and this change has been accompanied by an improvement in the general tone of politics. At the same time, most students of government would admit that the quality of candidates has not notably improved and that political machines, although less venal, still play a dominant role in the selection and election of these candidates.

Since it is obvious that "the right to elect is the right to select," it can be argued with force that new ways must be found to seek out better candidates and to see that they win nomination in the primaries. If good candidates are nominated by all parties, then it is inevitable that good candidates will be elected. On the other hand, if the November election offers the voters only a choice between Political Henchman A, selected by one boss, and Political Henchman B, selected by another boss, the democratic process becomes little more than a farce. The public is merely deluded into thinking that it has exercised a democratic right.

The direct primary is a step in the right direction, but only the politically naïve could conclude that this invention has purified politics of its baleful influences. The root of the trouble goes back to the spoils system, which was introduced during the Jacksonian era. The party system was permitted at that time to polarize about self-interest, rather than about principle or ideology, as had been largely true under earlier Presidents.

In the years since, the philosophy of what's-in-it-for-me has dominated American politics, as opposed to the idea that participation in government, either as voter or elected official, is a privilege and a service to be performed even at great personal sacrifice. Nowhere is the crass philosophy of self-interest more blatantly exposed than in the national party platforms, which spell out in detail the special inducement or bribe offered to every group and voting bloc in the country in return for its vote.

Because there is an obvious need to change the tone of politics and to find new and better ways of seeking out, and encouraging, the ablest persons to stand for office, it is worthwhile to examine in some detail just how candidates enter the lists today.

Normally a person becomes a candidate in either of two ways: by party selection, or by self-selection. Selection by party is a euphemism, as anyone can testify who has worked closely with a political machine. Seldom is a candidate chosen by the vote of rank-and-file party members, except in smaller communities, where members are known and where they can all assemble in one place. It is not the party members who typically select the candidates but the party boss, or the inner circle around him.

In making his selection, the party boss usually has two thoughts in mind: he wants to pick a candidate who can win, since his prestige and power are involved in being a successful boss, and he wants to choose a candidate who, win or lose, will remain loyal and work to bring to the machine the maximum in the way of patronage and spoils. In short, his choice goes to that candidate who will be loyal to the machine and who has the best chance of winning. Since few men of integrity are willing to make obeisance to politicians of this character, it is easy to understand why able persons do not wish to enter politics by this route.

The second route to politics—self-selection—is equally unappealing to those who are not self-advertisers. Modesty keeps many able persons from throwing their own hats into the political ring. More important, the independent, non-machine candidate faces a formidable task in trying to beat the party choice in the primary, because few citizens normally take the trouble to vote, while the machine can muster its followers easily. Because of these considerations, self-selection is not a popular way to enter politics, and the fact that its appeal all too often has been limited to political "nuts" has not increased its popularity.

Strangely, the procedure commonly followed by universities, business firms, and other institutions in filling vacancies where personnel of high caliber are needed is not used in politics. If a university wishes to find a new president, it certainly is not content to rest its selection on those who just happen to apply for the job. Instead, the trustees, or a group appointed by them, usually comb the country to find the most suitable man; and when he is found, they do their best to induce him to take the job. This is the same procedure that most large corporations follow in trying to find a president or other high-ranking officer. For the more important positions, the job seeks the man—the man does not seek the job.

Sooner or later the United States must devise a plan that recognizes this principle if it wishes to bring into public office a greater number of persons of high ability and character. The procedure need not be divorced from political party, and there is every reason to carry it out under the aegis of the party.

Many persons still argue that patronage and the spoils system are necessary to nourish and sustain the party system in America. This has never been proved; and the great strength of the party system in Great Britain, where the moral standards of politics are appreciably higher than in the United States, is strong evidence that parties need not rely on questionable sources of income to maintain their strength.

The Grand Delusion

Most Americans grow up in the belief that somewhere in the nation many persons, able and highly trained, are at work on solutions to the nation's most persistent problems, such as unemployment, labor relations, foreign aid, juvenile delinquency, agricultural surpluses, military defense, and the like. They have in mind the many thousands of persons attached to government and the additional thousands in universities and other institutions. The John and Mary Does comfort themselves with the thought that scores of talented individuals are giving their undivided thought to the cause and cure of our national ills.

Nothing could be farther from the truth. This is a grand delusion, which needs to be dispelled if what the public believes to be true is ever to be translated into actuality. There is no dearth of brilliant minds in government and in our other institutions, but few are ever free to devote more than part time to major problems. Thousands of persons putter away on the fringes of these problems, but amazingly few have the opportunity to deal with them in the whole. Because this is the case, the problems persist, and new and imaginative solutions fail to be produced in the number required.

The reasons for this situation are many. Probably the most important is the failure to invent the kind of organizational design that makes ample provision for thinking and planning, and which also assures that thinking and planning are undertaken under optimal conditions.

The larger the organization, the more likely it is to be plagued with dinosauritis—a disease that produces large bodies with small minds. Not only in Washington but throughout the business world, talented individuals in top positions become enmeshed with administration and find themselves sooner or later devoting all their waking hours and all their mental energy to the administrative details that every organization spawns. Often this burden is welcomed. America's philosophy from the earliest days has been to glorify action and not thinking. Making administrative decisions is proof of action; thinking is not so easily observable. Many heads of government departments, and many businessmen for that matter, get to their desks early in the morning and stay until late at night under the delusion that they are being effective in their jobs, whereas in fact they are only being active.

By the same token, the head of a government agency or the president of a business concern who announces to his associates that he is going to spend the next two weeks alone in the mountains or at the seashore, to detach himself from the pressure of dealing with routine details in order to think more clearly about the future, is put down as slightly unbalanced by some and as a work shirker by others.

The ever-present lure of administrative detail is not the only foe of thinking and planning. Another is the natural reluctance of Homo sapiens to concern himself with the heart or core of any problem as opposed to tangential aspects and details. Trivia have a strange lure, even to good minds. We smile when we think of the scholastics of the Middle Ages idling away their time trying to figure out how many angels could stand on the point of a needle. But much of the study and research today in American universities is of the same order, requiring not brains but only persistence.

Examples of the failure to think and to plan ahead could be drawn from many fields. In the case of military defense the errors are out in the open for all to see and, for this reason, fair game for the critics. Because these errors can be easily identified as such, and not because they are more glaring or greater in number than might be found in other fields of government, military departments have been chosen to show the need for a new kind of organization design or system that will provide fully for imaginative thinking and forward planning.

Arnold Toynbee insists that there is no case in history when a nation devised a new weapon or a new strategy that its enemy did not invent the next one. Since military establishments obviously attract their share of brilliant minds, the failure to produce, accept, and put into effect new ideas must rest with the structures of these organizations.

A brief review of recent decades will illustrate the kinds of mistakes that military establishments have made in the past and will continue to make in the future unless steps are taken to change the usual type of military organization. Such a review will also serve to show how one experiment, undertaken during World War II, may provide the answer as to how problems of the world can be dealt with more intelligently by the better utilization of the brains of men.

As the threat of Hitler and a new war loomed in Europe in the 1930's, leaders in charge of the nation's defense were forced to deal with the question of the future importance of air power. The American public expressed, through many surveys, its overwhelming approval of building up the defenses of the country, particularly the air force, and at the same time the people registered their willingness to pay the tax bill.

The military leaders, strange as it seems years later, were not at all convinced that air power would play an important role in the next war. In fact, they were so convinced of the contrary that six months after World War II had begun, they asked Congress to appropriate only enough money to build 1,200 military airplanes. Congress, even less convinced than the military leaders that airplanes were important, appropriated enough money to build just 59 planes! When America was plummeted into the war a year later, the marines had exactly 6 aircraft to defend Wake Island. Here is an interesting case in which the people, who are supposed to know little about the arts of war, possessed much greater insight than their military and congressional leaders.

A second example of failure to look ahead and plan accordingly came during the Korean War. When the Communists invaded South Korea, America's Defense Department had failed to anticipate the development in aircraft. Those in charge of defense were not ready to accept the fact that jet planes would supersede propeller-driven planes, even though the jet plane was by no means new at that time. A British air cadet, Frank Whittle, invented the jet engine in 1928; but it was not until the early stages of the second World War that the first jet propulsion engine was actually used in combat. In 1941, the day after the Houses of Parliament were bombed, a British Gloster plane made the first successful jet flight.

Although the experts had had many years to study the relative merits of the two types of planes, it was not until some time after hostilities had begun in Korea, when the superiority of the jet plane was obvious to all, that the United States set out to correct its error. Undoubtedly there were individuals in the Defense Department who believed all along that jet planes were better, but their views failed to carry weight.

A third example demonstrates again the need for a new kind of organizational design that can deal with new ideas and weapons. This example has to do with the failure to assess correctly the future possibilities of a weapon used in the later stages of World War II against England. The V2 rocket bombs created havoc; and if the war had not ended when it did—or if Hitler's planning department had given early priority to this new kind of missile—the effect upon British morale might have been a matter of grave concern.

The rockets that launched these bombs had been developed by German scientists. Their potentialities were grasped quickly by the Russians, and the long lead they established in this field after the war can only be accounted for by the failure of United States defense leaders and our allies to appraise correctly their future importance. Belatedly the United States is in the process of overcoming the early lead of the Russians. Again, however, the advance planning and thinking department was found wanting.

During the Korean War the Russians revealed a new strategy, which continues to be successful and which presents the United

States and its allies with a serious military problem. Until the end of the nineteenth century it was the custom for a few nations to make regular use of mercenaries. Russia has improved upon this idea. Since World War II the Russians have managed to fight wars in widely separated areas of the world—not with Russian troops—but with native troops trained by Russia. Russian soldiers did not man the front lines in Korea; the soldiers were North Koreans, and later Chinese, who had been skillfully trained, supplied, and indoctrinated by the Russians.

For two years the explanation offered by United States military leaders for not meeting this strategy with a similar strategy was that South Koreans could not be trained to be good fighters, at least in the time necessary. Not until late in the war was any serious effort made to train and equip the many hundreds of thousands of Koreans of military age who were ready and willing to engage in battle.

This strategy of the Russians continues to be used (in Cuba, Viet Nam, and elsewhere, as this is being written) and presents a tremendous threat, to which the Western nations have not yet adjusted or responded. Russia is in a position to start brush fires throughout the world, wherever and whenever Communist-indoctrinated troops in sufficient strength can be trained and supplied. The term "brush fire" was coined in America, and it is a good example of how language can deceive a whole nation. The term conveys the impression that the United States can move its forces quickly into a troubled area, settle successfully any dispute with small loss of life, avoid an all-out war, and bring its troops back home to wait until the next brush fire breaks out.

A more realistic examination of brush-fire wars points to this typical course of events. United States forces (with or without allies) engage the native troops armed by the Communists. Russia stays on the side line to watch developments. After the United States has become heavily committed, and before her forces can bring the war to a successful conclusion, Russia issues a manifesto. Either the United States calls a halt to its war efforts and reaches some accord with the native troops it faces, or it risks the entrance of Russia in an all-out war. Since the United States does not want a third world war, or to be charged with starting it, the United States and Russia engage in lengthy peace conversations, which end in a stalemate. Meanwhile, the United States does not dare withdraw all of its troops or reduce its financial support of the side it has come to defend. United States forces stay on for years, always fearful that the day help is withdrawn, the Communists may take over.

This is the pattern that has begun to repeat itself. It works to the great advantage of the Russians, who can disperse United States strength about the world, committing this nation to the expenditure of billions and billions of dollars for foreign aid and for the kind of weapons that would be relatively ineffective if used against Russia in an all-out war.

The final example has to do with an entirely new kind of warfare, fought with ideas and not bullets, yet for the same ultimate purpose —world supremacy. In this new kind of warfare there are no national boundaries to be honored and protected; the battlefield is the earth itself and all of its inhabitants.

The Russians saw the great possibilities in psychological warfare many years ago, and their knowledge of one of its instruments— propaganda—and their skill in using it have been demonstrated in all parts of the world. The United States has not yet become attuned to this kind of warfare and, as a result, has made little progress in using this means to win the battle for the minds of men.

The word *propaganda* frightens many Americans because it is associated with the deceit and treachery practiced by Nazi Germany and with the lack of good faith and honesty displayed daily by the Russians. Propaganda, to many, is synonymous with lying. However, the critics of propaganda overlook an all-important fact. Propaganda based upon truth can be even more effective in the long run than propaganda based upon lies. The shining example is Christianity. No other religion in the world has won so many converts, and none has so assiduously propagandized the people in every part of the globe. Missionaries have risked their lives in disease-ridden and primitive lands in their zeal to bring the Christian message to all of mankind. And Christianity has been extraordinarily effective, chiefly because its missionaries hold out the promise of a better life to the downtrodden and impoverished masses of the world.

It is not strange, therefore, that the Communists have achieved much success in the underdeveloped nations of the world by taking a lesson from Christianity. Only in their case, they hold out the prospect of improved economic conditions to the poor, who still unfortunately represent a vast majority of the inhabitants of the earth.

Prime Minister Nehru singled out, some years ago, the basic weakness in America's point of view. He said that in dealing with world problems, the Government of the United States was inclined to think solely in terms of military might, or in terms of money. To put it more bluntly and less diplomatically than Nehru, we try to get our way by threats or bribes. In his opinion we have overlooked the natural aspirations of people in other areas of the world, and we have neglected to give them a better understanding of our own point of view.

The Peace Corps represents a hopeful beginning, but it is on a scale so small as to be no match for the world-wide apparatus of the Communist party. There are no rules established yet in this new type of struggle, but at least at this stage of our knowledge we can apply one of the rules of a shooting war: we must reach more people, more often, and with a better and more effective message than our enemy. To do this will require some share of the billions now devoted to outmoded weapons and concepts of war, and it will require a staff, and thinking, commensurate with the global nature of the task.

Whether the anti-Communist nations like it or not, they are already in the midst of a world-wide ideological war, which must be fought as intelligently and as vigorously as a shooting war. In the case of the United States our information agency, the Voice of America, is most effective when it confines itself to the important function of supplying honest and believable news. Psychological warfare, on the other hand, should be undertaken by a new and independent agency.

The classic, schoolbook ideas of warfare must change to deal with the new realities. There are two kinds of warfare—not one—and to "win" requires that a nation gain supremacy in both. It must always be kept in mind that a nation can win a shooting war and, within a few years, lose or dissipate all the hoped-for gains by neglecting to convert the enemy to its ways of thinking. Conversely, a nation can lose a "hot" war but in the long run win by getting its ideas accepted.

Certainly students of history would have to agree that regardless of which nation or nations win or lose the wars that may come during the next hundred years, the side whose ideas are most widely accepted will prevail in the future.

Every department of government makes errors of many varieties. Military departments are probably no worse than others, but their mistakes, like those of pollsters, are more obvious. If other departments of government had to enter contests where one side won and the other lost, their faults would be exposed in the same pitiless manner.

The military leader who has devoted most of his military career to the tank corps and whose future is tied up with the importance and funds assigned his branch of the service will obviously resist any thought that the tank corps should be relegated to a less important position. Regardless of all evidence to the contrary, he will talk himself into believing that the tank corps will play an even more important future role.

Such convictions come about in a natural way and, in a certain sense, are admirable. At the same time it should not be forgotten that their effect is to make virtually certain that new ideas will never have a fair hearing.

The typical method followed in democracies for dealing with problems that revolve about self-interest is to reach a compromise through bargaining. Competing groups are brought together with the hope that each will give enough ground to enable a final settlement, acceptable to all, to be produced.

The weakness of this plan, when it is used by military establishments, is that it virtually guarantees that new ideas will not be accepted. The reason is the very basic one of money. There are never enough funds for the new as well as the old, and consequently the new is sacrificed because it has not had an opportunity to build up a vested interest.

If it is recognized that human beings whose loyalties and self-interest are deeply involved cannot be expected to pass judgment objectively upon a new idea, then it becomes a matter of good common sense to set up a kind of organizational pattern that takes account of this well-established and obvious fact. In the case of military establishments this means setting up a new kind of planning center, staffed by men who have no vested interest in or loyalty to any branch of the armed services and whose careers are not directly involved in the decisions made. Only in this manner can outmoded practices and weapons be eliminated, and new ideas given their full chance to prove themselves.

The Great Experiment

During World War II, the United States carried out one of the most successful ventures in the history of man—the making of an atom bomb. Apart from its obvious scientific and military value, the Manhattan Project (officially known as the Manhattan Engineer District), which carried out the experiment, demonstrated what men working in concert under optimum conditions can achieve when their talents are fully employed.

In the years since World War II, the threat to man from nuclear explosions has tended to obscure the great contribution of this project to the advancement of mankind. It proved, among other things, that it is possible for men working together to realize some of the great potentialities of collective action.

This truth is being demonstrated in many fields today: in medical science, where researchers are working in teams to isolate the virus of cancer and many other diseases; in the production of new drugs; in the making of missiles and satellites; and in many other enterprises. The uniqueness of the approach can be illustrated by contrasting the manner in which the Manhattan Project proceeded with the task of constructing an atom bomb, and the fate which might have befallen it had usual procedures been followed.

First, let us suppose that secrecy had not been important and that the construction of an atom bomb had been forced to run the usual gamut of military and congressional approval. The account, of course, must be entirely speculative, but it serves a purpose.

The first question that would have to be settled, once the proposal to make an atom bomb had been made, would be the matter of money. Any large appropriation would have to be approved by Congress, and before any money could be, or would be, approved, the question of whether the United States should try to make a bomb would obviously be thoroughly debated.

While this debate was going on in Congress, it is a safe guess that the various branches of the military service would make rival claims for building and controlling the use of the bomb. Meanwhile, it would be only normal to expect much opposition from military sources, particularly if approval of the bomb meant depriving the regular services of funds they thought necessary.

Congressional approval would be difficult to obtain. As soon as it was established that huge sums of money would be necessary, opposition would arise on this score alone. However, assuming that Congress finally accepted the plan, then competition would start to locate plants in the districts or states where members of Congress saw a political advantage from the money to be spent and the new jobs to be created.

As soon as the debate got underway as to the location of the plant facilities for building the bomb, the congressmen representing districts where conventional weapons of war were being produced might be expected to take fright, especially when they realized that the new project, if successful, might have the ultimate effect of lessening the demand for old weapons and reducing thereby the payrolls in their districts and states. With loss in employment would come loss in popularity for the incumbent congressman and his party. This threat would be sufficient to stir some into questioning whether the right decision had been made to attempt to make the bomb at all.

As this debate was carried on, opposition to the project would begin to crystallize. The cry would go up that since the whole plan was in the experimental stage, it was wrong to ask the already heavily burdened taxpayer to put up money for a venture the success of which was so uncertain. Moreover, many other departments of the service could use a lot more money on the conventional weapons of warfare.

The more the issue of making the bomb, and the money it would entail, were argued, the more would congressional pressures build up to delay the whole idea. The ultimate result of this process could be predicted with a high degree of certainty: the money, if appropriated at all, would be only enough to carry on experimentation on a small scale, and the approval of the full amount of funds needed would not assure the completion of the bomb within the time requirements.

To those who insist that this type of bickering and bargaining are the price a nation must pay for democracy, there is a simple answer. Inefficiency and inability to plan ahead are not essential features of the democratic process. They exist only because democratic societies have failed to invent new systems and practices that make it possible for men to work at the highest level of their ability.

Modern societies must concern themselves with a whole array of problems that could not possibly have been anticipated by the founding fathers. Those who framed America's Constitution dealt with the problems of their day with extraordinary insight; but the problems of their day are only a part of the problems of this era. Even though they were political inventors of the highest order, and their methods have served America well in many areas, they could not foresee, and provide for, effective ways to deal with the special kinds of problems that have arisen nearly two hundred years later.

No one understood this better than Franklin D. Roosevelt. When the project of producing an atom bomb was accepted by him, he did everything he could to circumvent both Congress and the military establishment. General Leslie Groves, who headed the Manhattan Project, makes this statement in his book *Now It Can Be Told*: "For reasons of military security, we had always made a determined effort to withhold all information on the atomic bomb project from everyone, including members of the Executive department, military personnel and members of Congress, except those who definitely needed it and were authorized to receive it. As a result our methods of obtaining funds had always been rather unorthodox."

Democratic procedures must constantly be brought up to date, which means that political invention is just as important today as it was in 1787. The framers of the Constitution could not foresee the nature of the problems America would face in the future, but they had enough foresight to provide for change.

No society can remain static, and the procedures that are effective in one era will almost certainly not be equally effective in the next. A constant search must be conducted to find new ways to solve new problems. The Manhattan Project found a new and important way —however some may regret the result.

Problem Solving by Group Action

Specific features of the team effort used in the Manhattan Project need to be pointed out to provide a clearer idea of how the amazing feat of making the first atom bomb was achieved in so short a time.

The scientists and other personnel who took part in the project were selected solely on the basis of the contribution they might be expected to make. No attempt was made to "balance" the group by choosing Republicans and Democrats, including Catholics, Protestants, and Jews, or making sure that different regions of the country were represented. No one was put on the staff to pay a political debt.

Because of wartime secrecy, the project was highly classified and the persons who directed the experiment were not identified in the press or in any other public manner. Many benefits flowed from this anonymity. There was no urge—and in fact no opportunity—to air grievances or differences of opinion, to seek publicity for themselves or for the project. The press and other media of communication were not in a position, inadvertently or otherwise, to widen any breaches that may have existed among the personnel, particularly between the military personnel on the one hand and the scientists on the other. No one had publicly to justify any decision or any point of view.

The task at hand could be prosecuted without thought as to whether its success would benefit the Army more than the Navy, or the Navy more than the Air Force. No one had to worry about the credit that would redound to management or labor, or whether the experiment would prove Professor A's theories right and Professor B's theories wrong.

Since the goal was to help win the war and bring the fighting to an earlier close, there was constant pressure to get on with the job and not to waste time quarreling over protocol or debating minor details. The work itself was carried out with a minimum of the usual distractions that beset workers in metropolitan centers. In fact, the physical isolation of the laboratories and manufacturing facilities at Oak Ridge, Hanford, and Los Alamos helped reduce the competition from normal interests and pursuits.

The success achieved by this unique effort leads naturally to the question as to whether some of the special features of the approach can be utilized in dealing with other problems. Specifically, can the team approach, on a far less ambitious scale, be useful in helping to alleviate such problems as crime, unemployment, racial tensions, disarmament, and the many others that assume particular importance today?

Many organizations and groups have concerned themselves with these problems, both at the national and local levels. Their efforts, although eminently worthwhile, have not been attended with much success. It is therefore pertinent to inquire into the probable reasons for this lack of success. Such an inquiry should prove as enlightening in guiding future efforts as the examination of the reasons for the outstanding success of the Manhattan Project.

The committee method for solving problems has never acquired much prestige. Moreover, congressional committees have not added to the luster of this approach. Standing committees of Congress are usually overshadowed by their chairmen, who have extraordinary powers; and the investigating committees are usually appointed mostly to gain publicity for members and to further political ends. Generally their aim is to prove something, not to find the truth and be guided accordingly. This is not to say that good has not come from many of their investigations. Nevertheless, whatever the motive in appointing the committee, the findings can never be divorced from political considerations and for this reason are always suspect.

Although the committee method is generally held in low repute as a means of solving problems, there is no reason why this should be the case. Group action can be effective in producing recommendations and solutions, and the chief reason why this type of action is not more highly regarded is the lack of skill and experience in knowing how to deal with such bodies.

This fact has been convincingly demonstrated by Frank C. Moore, former Lieutenant Governor of the state of New York and president of the Government Affairs Foundation. His amazing accomplishments with citizens' committees in finding solutions to difficult local and state problems negate the prevailing low opinion of what committees can achieve. Governor Moore's experience shows how government and society can resolve many of their most complicated problems when the mental abilities and energies of small groups are carefully channeled and the conditions under which they carry on their deliberations are properly organized. The problems with which Governor Moore's committees have dealt range all the way from state fiscal assistance to localities, to the modernizing of provisions of New York's state constitution and the recommendation of new constitutional amendments. The great success of the committees is attested by the fact that virtually every statutory change proposed during an entire decade was passed by the legislature and approved by the governor, with little or no partisan disagreement, and every constitutional change was approved not only by the legislature but subsequently by the people themselves.

Governor Moore's experience in working with committees brings out many basic principles that must be recognized if similar worthwhile achievements are to be expected. They can best be summarized in a list of *do's* and *don'ts*.

1. Don't ask any advisory committee of citizens to deal with an easy problem. These committees are more successful when they concern themselves with difficult ones, especially those that official agencies have been unable to solve.

2. Don't coax anyone to serve, or accept anyone as a member of

the committee unless he agrees to attend every meeting and to give his full effort.

3. Avoid choosing persons who stand to profit personally from the committee's action, or who have to clear their votes with any organization they may represent.

4. It is not necessary to select persons who are expert or even especially well-informed about the problem under study, provided that they are intelligent, objective, and favorably known to a substantial segment of the persons concerned with the problem.

5. The number of members to include can vary, but experience in New York State would indicate that fifteen is a workable and effective number.

6. Committee meetings should be held at a place that is not too comfortable or attractive, and they should be free of the diversions usually offered by palatial country clubs and summer resorts.

7. At the first two or three committee meetings basic, factual information should be presented through a series of carefully prepared memoranda, which are later supplied to all members. To make certain that every member is familiar with the content, the memoranda should be read aloud to the entire committee.

8. The first meetings should be designed solely to clarify the understanding of committee members. In this process, as Governor Moore states, "It has always been amazing to see how problems diminish in size and complexity as the actual facts are disclosed and understood."

9. After the presentation of the facts has been completed (which may require several meetings), the discussion should begin—but not before this time. At the conclusion of each of the later meetings the chairman should review and "peg down" the points upon which agreement has been reached, keeping for later discussion the points of disagreement.

10. From the beginning to the end of the committee's task, the chairman should not forget that the goal is the solution of the problem and not the writing of a report "to be abandoned, like a foundling child, on the doorstep of some other agency."

11. The report should be designed with the thought in mind to broaden the knowledge and understanding of the problem on the part of public officials and citizens and "to encourage and equip the authorized agencies to take effective action upon the recommendations of the committee."

12. The report that emerges should be as attractive and as readable as it can be made. It should be written in clear, concise language with avoidance of "officialese." It should be distributed widely. The salient points in the report itself can be supplied to the newspapers and other media of communication as soon as the committee has reached agreement on the findings.

Here, then, is a practical plan for solving by group action those problems that beset local communities and states. Governor Moore's experience supplies proof enough that this can be done. And it does more: it proves, in Moore's own words, "Advisory committees provide almost limitless opportunities for effective participation of citizens in their government at all levels."

The Shortcomings of Conferences
and Similar Gatherings

Most meetings are little more than an organized waste of time. What is said in hours can usually be read in minutes, assuming that it is worth even this much time. Certainly there have been few attempts to plan and organize these gatherings, even of top-level persons, so as to settle or solve problems or even to give those who attend a better understanding of some new development. In the main, the typical program retains all the faults of the bits-and-pieces type of approach to learning embodied in the classroom-lecture system.

Oddly enough, the yearly meetings arranged by scholars display no more ingenuity than do the annual outings of the West Side Clam Bake Society, and certainly they are more boring. The custom of reading papers based upon the latest bit of trivia unearthed by library research is hardly calculated to stimulate the higher brain centers.

Where there is no formal program and the meeting, or conference, is built around "discussion groups," the odds are great that a few bores will do all the discussing and what others contribute will be for effect's sake.

Many conferences, of course, have no loftier aim than to give members a chance to get away from home (with expenses paid or tax deductions allowed) and to offer a pleasant rendezvous with friends. On the more practical side, such meetings often serve as a market place for job hunters and contact seekers.

One of the most colorful descriptions of the modern conference comes from W. Grey Walter, who wrote: "The number of international and inter-disciplinary symposia, colloquia, conferences, congresses, study groups, and seminars is already far too great for comfort and efficiency even in the age of jet transport. A conscientious and fluent scientist could spend his whole time attending meetings and editing transcripts of his remarks. A new scientific type is emerging, the Conference Man, with bulging brief-case, drip-dry shirt, and many visaed passport. Most easily observable in airport waiting rooms, he occasionally reappears in his laboratory to replenish his stock of lantern slides with startling discoveries regurgitated by his less mobile colleagues."

The conduct of business meetings also needs the attention of those who would reduce the amount of time that highly trained and busy persons must waste in observing hoary rituals.

A meeting of otherwise intelligent persons can be reduced to a snarling group of human beings by endless arguments as to whether one motion takes precedence over another, whether Jones or Smith should be recognized by the chairman, whether a motion should or should not be tabled, whether this word or that should be struck out of a resolution.

Parliamentary law serves a valuable purpose in providing for the orderly conduct of business brought before deliberative assemblies, and for the protection of the rights of majorities as well as minorities. It is only when these elaborate rules, which may be important for legislative bodies, are adopted by groups whose purpose is quite different that the end result is often to defeat the very purpose for which the rules were intended.

If the purpose of such rules is to provide for the expeditious conduct of meetings, to bring out the best thinking of those present, to delineate areas of agreement and engineer consent, to make progress toward the solution of the problems under discussion, then a new set of rules should be devised for nonlegislative bodies. Parliamentary law is patently not suited for nonparliamentary groups.

Royal Commissions of Inquiry

For centuries Great Britain has had its Royal Commissions of Inquiry, which have been described as "a typically English device for bringing the best brains of the country to bear on legislative tasks." In marked contrast to congressional committees, which "exhibit a definitely partisan and political bias alike in their membership, their proceedings, and their reports," Royal Commissions attempt to approach problems in a strictly impartial manner and "not on the plane of propaganda."

Royal Commissions have been used to investigate, and to make legislative recommendations, on a wide variety of problems ranging from lotteries, old-age pensions, health insurance, the operation of the courts, to the state of the fine arts and the problems of university education. In fact, almost every problem of major importance has been the subject of investigation by a Royal Commission.

To be named a member of a Royal Commission has always been regarded as a great distinction. It is undoubtedly for this reason that the British Government has never had the least difficulty in finding important and influential persons who are willing to serve in an unpaid capacity on these commissions, although the work often requires months of effort and time.

Royal Commissions are completely independent. They can follow their own rules, and they can carry on their deliberations for a few months or for years. The number of persons making up the commissions ranges usually from five to twenty-one.

The type of personnel selected depends to a great extent upon the problem. Persons selected to serve can be experts in a given field; they can represent specific bodies involved in the investigation; or they can be citizens, chosen for their proven integrity and impartiality and known for their sound judgment. Significantly, commissions composed of this latter type of member have generally been most successful.

Although fewer Royal Commissions have been appointed during recent decades than in earlier periods of British history, there has been a great proliferation in the number of national advisory committees. Royal Commissions, created to deal with a specific problem, come to an end when their work is completed and a report issued. Advisory committees are typically of a standing character, although some are temporary.

The great use to which the various departments of Great Britain's central government puts these committees is revealed in the following figures. In the year 1958, a total of 484 committees of a standing nature were in existence. This total reaches the remarkable number of 850 when committees of a temporary nature are included.

In many respects the advisory committees resemble Royal Commissions. Members are typically appointed by the various ministers; they receive no pay for their services, except on those occasions when much time of specialists and experts is required. Advisory committees deal largely with subjects of importance to Parliament to which this body cannot give adequate attention.

The executive and legislative departments of the Federal Government of the United States and the central government of Great Britain are faced with similar problems in dealing with those matters that affect the self-interest of important groups. In dealing with such problems, the two nations have evolved entirely different procedures. In the United States, lobbyists representing pressure groups do their special pleading before members of Congress individually or before committees of Congress. The larger and more influential organizations have their own buildings and offices in Washington and make use of every legitimate (and often illegitimate) way to influence legislation in their favor. Since in most fields competing interests are to be found, it can be argued that the work of one group merely offsets or nullifies that of another. This is not true, however, when one group is exceptionally well-organized and can muster its members at the polls to help elect or defeat a given congressman.

From time to time attempts have been made to control lobbyists and to minimize their power. Still they flourish, as the constantly increasing number of Washington offices representing special-interest groups bears ample witness. Of course, not all the efforts of pressure groups are to be condemned. Often they make themselves useful to members of Congress by providing them with information that might not otherwise come to their attention.

By contrast, the device of advisory committees in Great Britain has made this type of lobbying unnecessary. The important and competing organizations in any one field normally are represented on the advisory committee dealing with the legislative and policy problems of that specific area. Each organization, therefore, has a fair and full opportunity to present its views to the committee.

A report by the Political and Economic Planning Group (PEP) has this to say about advisory committees in its special report on these groups: "They [advisory committees] involve interest groups, but their form and their purpose make reasoned argument the best weapon at the groups' disposal; the strength of a case can count for something in these circumstances as well as the power of the organizations. Advisory committees proceed by discussion and compromise, by argument and agreement; they constitute policy-making machinery for government at low temperature."

Each branch of the Congress of the United States has its many standing committees. Laymen, experts, and representatives of special-interest groups are usually asked to appear before these committees when proposed legislation is being considered. Although there can be little doubt that most congressmen approach service on these committees with a high sense of responsibility and a genuine desire to get at the facts and make fair judgments, the political character of the committees introduces a prejudicial factor, which can never be entirely removed, especially on highly controversial issues. In Great Britain similar committees of Parliament, called Select Committees, are rarely used because of this failing.

Most problems need to be considered in a calm atmosphere, where both the strong and the weak have the same opportunity to be heard and where competing interests can place their case before impartial persons, whose task is to come to reasonable and fair decisions that take account of the public's interest. Such a system does away with the need and the cost of expensive lobbying operations and removes the coercion to which members of Congress are all too often subjected.

Legislation that is free of political taint and that is not unduly influenced by the stronger and more aggressive pressure groups at the expense of the less well-organized is almost certain to prove better and more lasting.

A New Way to Solve National Problems

We return again to the very basic conclusion that man has great and largely unrealized potentialities. In the light of the experience reported it is now clear that working in concert, and under carefully organized conditions, men can collectively work wonders.

Amazingly little attention has been devoted to the best ways of utilizing the tremendous intellectual powers of mankind. We stumble along, aware of the shortcomings of present systems and institutions but without the urge to change or improve them, or even the conviction that something can be done.

Little imagination and mental effort are required to analyze efforts of the past that have been notably successful. Factors common to the successful can be identified as readily as those common to the unsuccessful. This is one of the simplest of all analytical processes and perhaps the most ignored in all departments of life.

Examination of the procedures described earlier, in which group action achieved great success, permits us to draw up a detailed pattern for future efforts. It would be foolhardy to regard such a plan as representing anything more than a starting point. If this is kept in mind, the steps can now be described which group action should follow in dealing with the great problems of our era.

1. *The team approach.* The greatest success has been achieved when a fairly small group—usually ten to twenty individuals—works

together as a team, with each person having a definite contribution to make in furthering the effort.

2. *Selection of members.* Of key importance, the selection of members should be put in the hands of a competent but nonpolitical committee, which might be composed of university presidents. The university presidents could be selected by some such organization as the American Philosophical Society, or a similar organization that enjoys a high reputation for integrity and public interest.

The actual selection of members of the group should be based upon these general qualifications: (a) special training or background that has some applicability to the problem; (b) demonstrated capacity for original thinking; (c) objectivity as applied both to themselves and to their work; (d) reputation for sound judgment and impartiality.

Persons to be excluded from consideration should be: (a) those who are too closely attached to a pressure or self-interest group identified with the problem under investigation; (b) those who already are committed to a particular point of view; (c) those whose jobs and future might be jeopardized by any conclusion inimical to their own profession.

3. *Anonymity.* The names of persons selected should not be publicized until after the report has been made. Obviously, all group discussions and the views espoused by any one person should be kept strictly confidential.

4. *Isolation.* To avoid competing interests, and to permit the group to work continuously and without interruption, a meeting place removed from a large city or a similar place of attraction should be chosen. A pleasantly located hotel run well enough to allow members to think about their work—and not about the service—would probably best meet the needs of the group.

5. *Recompense.* Members should have all of their out-of-pocket expenses paid, but should receive no remuneration over and above this. Membership on the committee should be regarded strictly as a service to the country; and the business, industry, or educational institution that releases a member of its staff for this purpose should

do so also as a contribution to the public welfare. The reward to members for serving on the committee might take the form of recognition on a Presidential Honors List.

6. *Problems to be investigated.* In the beginning, there should be no restriction whatsoever as to the problems to be investigated, the only test being that a problem of importance exists and that the nation needs help in its solution. Some of the problems that can profitably be studied are: growth in crime, defense needs of the nation, juvenile delinquency, racial tension, unemployment, health and hospital insurance, veterans' benefits, agricultural surpluses and subsidies, employer-employee relations, the effects of automation, military planning, psychological warfare, foreign aid, local, state, and national taxation, industrial growth, improvements in education at all levels, changes in the electoral system, disarmament, housing and slum clearance, water shortage, air and water pollution, the aging population, public transportation, conservation, recreation, public health, cultural facilities, adult education, the prison system, the courts and justice, world peace, highway safety, divorce laws, and government economy. Other problems can be added to this list as they take on importance to the country.

7. *The gathering of factual data.* An all-important aspect of this approach is the careful gathering of all pertinent facts before the group has assembled. A full-time secretary should be given the responsibility for assembling all relevant information on the problem being studied. The material to be given to members of the group should be prepared in the form of written memoranda. The material assembled should include factual and statistical data regarding the current status of the problem, as well as all the theories and proposals for dealing with it. In short, the material would cover all the important and relevant facts that are available and all of the suggestions that have been advanced as to the best way of dealing with the problem.

The importance of this phase of problem solving cannot be overemphasized. Many conferences composed of persons of great talent have failed because those who participated were not thoroughly briefed on the facts and current status of the conference subject. Discussion is futile if one participant starts from one basis of fact, and another from an entirely different basis.

Still another good reason for producing a complete statement of the problem, and all the important views relating to it, is to have this information at hand when the final report is being prepared. On most of the important problems facing the nation, there is no single source of information that is brief, understandable, and suitable for general distribution.

8. *Procedure.* The first few days should be devoted to making certain that all are thoroughly informed. If there is disagreement on any point, this should be cleared up before going farther.

After the group has been briefed on all the significant facts, the next goal should be to free their minds and stimulate their imaginations as to possible solutions. At this stage the aim should be to break the chains of custom, explore new and novel ideas, and spur the individual members of the group to do their best original thinking.

When ample time has been given to the development of new hypotheses, or alternatives, the group can then settle down to the task of deciding which are worth pursuing further. Finally, when this has been done, the group should be in a position to lay out a course of action.

9. *Time requirements.* Groups do their best work when they are under pressure of time. Pressure keeps the discussion on the track, so that time is not wasted on unimportant details. A period of three or four weeks of concentrated effort is better than months spent in desultory discussion. After a time human beings run out of ideas, and when the stimulation that arises from original thinking is gone, little progress can be expected. The odds are great that if some plan of action has not been developed at the end of three or four weeks, it is unlikely that one will be forthcoming at all.

10. *Appointment of new teams.* If, after a reasonable period of time, the group finds that it can make no further progress, and it is unable to make any real contribution toward the solution of the

problem in question, then it should be dissolved and another group appointed to see if it can succeed where the first one failed. Some problems are of such compelling importance that a whole series of such efforts are fully warranted. Team after team might be necessary in dealing with the more complex problems, each team, in a sense, starting where the other left off.

In short, the team concept permits great flexibility. Many groups can be at work at the same time on a wide variety of problems, and certainly this type of group effort should be continued indefinitely— if their contribution turns out to be as great as experience indicates.

11. *Reporting the conclusions.* The conclusions reached by each group should receive wide publicity. In addition to supplying all media of communication with the full report, copies should be placed in the hands of all legislative bodies in the country and sent to all schools and colleges in the nation. Copies should be available for the public, through newsstands and other outlets.

The report, as stated earlier, should be a complete statement of the problem, the relevant facts and opinions about it, the issues involved, and the committee's findings and recommendations. Obviously it should be prepared in a way to make it understandable to persons in all walks of life. It should be physically attractive and easy to read. Dissenting views should be reported, if there are any and if they are important, along with reasons why they failed of adoption by the majority.

12. *Applying the findings.* Since this whole effort is designed to bring enlightenment to voters and help to legislative bodies, including Congress, there is no intent to expropriate legislative responsibilities. Legislative bodies should be completely free to act, or not to act, upon the recommendations. It can be assumed that if the findings make good sense to the public, then pressures will be brought to bear upon their representatives to adopt them. And the latter, being good citizens, should welcome any help from any source that enables the nation to deal more intelligently with its major problems.

13. *How much money is required?* Each team project would re-

quire an estimated outlay of $50,000 to $75,000, depending chiefly upon the time the team spent in session, the amount of advance preparation needed, and the character of the report. This money could come from foundations, public subscription, or the government itself.

14. *What results might be expected?* It is virtually certain that the best minds of America, put to work on the nation's most vexing problems, under the conditions best suited for thinking, should produce workable solutions to many, if not most, of our nation's difficulties.

In terms of money, the risk is small and the chances great for effecting savings of substantial amounts. The Defense Department of the United States spends an average of $140,000,000 every day of the year. Agricultural subsidies require approximately $13,000,000 a day; just the storage of surplus crops alone costs $3,000,000 a day. The cost to the public of increased crime and juvenile delinquency is difficult to estimate, but the cost to taxpayers most certainly runs into billions each year.

A conservative estimate of the amount of money that can be saved the nation, through better solutions arrived at by the methods outlined here, is considerable. With a federal budget running at about one hundred billion dollars annually, it is not too optimistic to expect that at least one-fourth to one-third of this amount can be saved if legislative bodies put into effect the recommendations of these teams.

The saving of even considerable amounts of money is, in the long run, of secondary importance. The chief concern should be to solve many of man's present worries, and eventually to lift him to a higher plane of civilization. If this project for making better use of man's great mental powers is successful on a national level, the way will be open to use the same method in solving those questions of an international character—questions such as the problem of world population growth, world health standards, international trade, educational standards, and finally the question of world peace itself.

We must now face up to the very real possibility that, through a strange combination of experiences ranging all the way from Royal Commissions in Great Britain, through the work of Governor Moore in New York State, to the making of the first atom bomb, we have at long last found a promising method for solving many of society's most onerous problems.

Facing a somewhat similar situation three hundred years ago, Bacon made this plea for the experimental method, which has been responsible for so much of man's great scientific progress since that time: "For there is no comparison between what we may lose by not trying and by not succeeding; since by not trying we throw away the chance of an immense good; by not succeeding we only incur the loss of a little human labor."

PART IV

THE NEW METHODOLOGY

The Importance of Methodology

It may seem strange to a layman that a method could play an important part in the march of civilization, but such is the case. Brain power, no matter how great, can accomplish little unless properly directed. The prehistory of the human race is ample proof of this. For thousands and thousands of years primitive man made almost no progress because he did not know how to use his intelligence. Except for two relatively brief periods prior to the Renaissance, even Western man advanced little for that very reason.

Not until Francis Bacon appeared on the scene was much thought given to the invention of knowledge as opposed to its cultivation. Bacon argued strenuously for an entirely new approach to the physical world. He would cast aside the teachings of the philosophers and the logicians and their ways of thinking and adopt, in their stead, a new approach to knowledge. He advocated the experimental approach, its virtue being that every finding and conclusion could be tested. Since every new bit of knowledge was demonstrably true, there would be no room for quarreling schools of thought, and knowledge about the physical world could be rapidly expanded. Bacon's foresight has proved correct. The world of knowledge, as a result, has been literally transformed by this special way of channeling man's intelligence. Almost all of the physical and material benefits mankind enjoys today are a product of this method of science.

The experimental method is one way to create knowledge and

understanding. There now looms in the offing a new method, which promises to make almost as great a contribution to man's social life as the experimental method has made to his material progress.

To understand the new concepts and procedures, it is important to understand the scientific, or experimental, method, which has played so important a part in the progress of Western civilization during the last three hundred years, particularly during the last few decades. Probably the simplest way to describe the scientific method is to say that it consists of "the direct questioning of nature by systematic observation and experiment." The method is comparatively easy to apply to those problems that lie within the province of physical science. As will be pointed out later, more complex and sophisticated methods are required to deal with social problems, and new concepts must be embraced and new procedures employed.

When the scientific method is applied to the problems of the physical world, the results are susceptible of demonstration and proof. In fact, the essence of the experimental method is that the predicted result must be obtained with each repetition of the experiment. When this method is applied to social problems—to people and not to physical matter—proof is not so easily established, and exact repetition of an experiment is often impractical or impossible. In short, people and conditions change, and as they change, so do the findings.

This is the dilemma the student faces when he tries to apply the experimental method to man's social existence and to the many problems of his mental life. There is a steady progression away from certainty as the conditions of the experiment become more difficult to control and as more variables are introduced. To illustrate different applications of the experimental method in situations in which reliable proof or validation becomes progressively more difficult to achieve, four examples have been chosen. They will illustrate the difficulties of the experimental approach.

First, it may be helpful to point out the steps in the classic scientific procedure:

1. The specific problem is identified, that is, defined and delineated.
2. The experimenter gathers all available data.
3. The facts are analyzed and classified.
4. Hypotheses are developed and studied.
5. Experiments are conducted to test the hypotheses.
6. The results of the experiments "prove" or "disprove" the hypotheses, or in any event, shed light on them.

The results of one experiment often point to the need for another. In the words of John S. Waugh, "It has been characteristic of all science that each new theoretical insight has led to new experiments, and the new experiments, in turn, have produced unexpected observations, which formed the basis for fresh theoretical speculation."

Oddly enough, man himself becomes an important factor in the process. Acceptance of the findings becomes a variable. Some men will accept the findings; others, presented with the same results, will not accept them.

To illustrate how the scientific method is applied and typical reactions to the findings, the following experiments are presented. They serve merely as illustrations, not as actual scientific experiments, for the obvious reason that a full description of the procedures and the results would require far more space than is available here.

Example Number One. A machine tool company wishes to find a better alloy for drills to be used with metals of exceptional hardness. As new and stronger metals are developed, better and harder tools must be found. The specific problem in this case is to find a better alloy to use in the drills that must bore through these new metals.

The experimenters decide, after reviewing the latest findings bearing upon the problem, that the addition of three new chemicals to present alloys holds promise for making the new drills superior to present ones. After further study it is decided on the basis of theoretical considerations that one of the three chemicals is likely to be the best. Drills are therefore made of the new compound.

In the actual experiment a dozen new drills are tested along with the best of the present drills. The hardest of the new metals is used in the test, and it is decided that the time taken for the drill to penetrate the metal, along with a microscopic examination of the wear on the cutting edges, will constitute the criteria for judging the superiority of the drills made of the new alloy.

The new drills prove superior to the old ones in every instance— and on both counts. There is, consequently, little reason to question the findings; and if there were the slightest doubt, the same experiment could be repeated dozens of times until all reasonable doubt is removed.

The conditions under which the test was conducted were rigorously controlled, and evidence of superiority is convincing. The experimental method has been employed under ideal circumstances, not the least of which is the degree of mental certainty attached to the findings. Everyone is satisfied. Definite progress has been made.

Example Number Two. In this next application of the experimental method the conditions cannot be controlled so rigorously and the degree of acceptance, perforce, is not so complete. The example has to do with diet.

The question has arisen as to which kind of shortening will add the greatest weight in a given period of time. After a study of all the existing data on this point, it is decided to try an experiment using rats as the subjects of the test. It is further decided that a diet consisting only of margarine will be fed the rats and that a period of ten days will be fixed for the duration of the experiment. The margarines are made of varying mixtures of butter, corn, oil, cottonseed oil, and soybean oil.

A total of sixty rats are used in the test: twenty are fed on combination A, twenty on combination B, and twenty on combination C. An exactly equal amount is fed to each of the three groups. The rats are weighed at the beginning and at the end of the test. Furthermore, all have the same heredity.

At the end of the ten-day period it is found that the rats fed on combination B have gained most weight—but only when the total weight gained by all twenty in this group is compared with the total weight gained by the other two groups fed the other two margarines. In fact, five of the twenty rats fed combination B have made the least gain of all, even though the over-all weight gain for the rats in this group exceeded the other two.

The conclusion is reached that, on the average, a diet consisting of combination B fed to rats for a period of ten days will add more weight than will combination A or C. There are, however, some doubts and misgivings about the findings and their application to human beings. What would happen if the period of the test were lengthened or shortened? Why did some of the rats fed on combination B fail to make the least gain? It was noted during the experiment that the rats which ate combination C devoured this margarine much more rapidly than did the rats in the other two groups. What significance can be attached to this?

Assailed by these and other doubts, the followers of the experiment are not quite certain what the experiment proved, and therefore they are not quite so happy about the results.

Example Number Three. The next example moves still farther into the area of uncertainty. This time the experiment deals directly with people and not with animals or physical matter. The conditions of the experiment are even more difficult to control than in the experiment dealing with diet. Moreover, the number of variables that have to be taken into account has increased.

The problem this time is to determine the effectiveness of a new drug that has been developed to reduce high blood pressure. After much laboratory work carried on by a team of researchers, an ethical pharmaceutical company has produced a new prescription, which it believes to be effective and which it wishes to submit to test.

The director of the experiment obtains the co-operation of three hospitals and their medical staffs. A total of seventy-five patients are divided into three groups, each containing the same number of chronic cases. The first group of twenty-five is given the new drug for a period of three weeks. The second group is used as a control group. The third group is given an inactive substance called a placebo to weigh the effects of any psychological factor that may (and frequently does) lead persons who receive a drug to imagine some benefit and, as a result of this psychosomatic factor, actually to show improvement.

At the beginning and end of the period the blood pressure of all the persons making up the three groups is taken, to evaluate the effects of the new drug. In the first group of twenty-five cases, ten are found who benefit greatly, five show some improvement, and the remaining ten show no change at all.

After examining the blood pressure of the placebo group, it is discovered that eight have shown slight improvement. In the control group there has been no significant change. On the basis of this evidence it is concluded that the new drug is probably effective and that it may help some persons suffering from high blood pressure. But again the experiment leaves many points in doubt. Why did some persons benefit and others not? Were the groups actually comparable, or did the group receiving the new drug differ in certain unobservable respects from the other two groups? What would happen if the test were repeated in other hospitals? Would the drug be as effective on nonhospitalized cases as on chronic cases?

As a result of the experiment there is a feeling that some progress has been made in the field, but because of the many variables there is a conviction that more tests are needed and that actual experience with the drug, in the hands of the medical profession, is essential before the findings can be fully accepted. People cannot be manipulated, or paired off, as easily as rats; and rats in turn cannot be controlled as easily as matter.

Example Number Four. In this final example the uncertainties increase and for the same reasons, namely, that test conditions cannot be carefully controlled and the greater number of variables entering the experiment cannot be so easily weighed or held constant.

This time the experiment concerns the effectiveness of a new way to increase the speed of reading. The experiment is conducted with junior high school students in a city with a population of 500,000. Four junior high schools are selected for the test, while four others in somewhat comparable neighborhoods are used as controls. One class of twenty-five students in the eighth grade is chosen in each of the four schools where the new method is to be tested. It is arranged that instruction by the new system be carried on for a period of one semester.

Before the experiment is begun, all students are given a test for speed of reading together with a comprehension test of material read. As for the experiment itself, a total of one hundred students are given forty minutes of instruction twice each week for a period of eighteen weeks. The control group follows the usual school program, with no particular attention given to their reading habits.

At the end of the semester the students given the special instruction show an average improvement in their reading speed of fifty words per minute. The control group has improved during the semester, but only to the extent of ten words per minute. After the results of the comprehension test are taken into account, it is concluded that the new method probably has merit. However, analysis of the figures raises many disquieting questions. For instance, about half of the students given the special instruction show only slight improvement. The question that creates the greatest doubt is whether the same amount of time devoted to improving the reading habits of the control group by the usual and present methods might not produce gains of the same order. In short, is the gain in speed due to the extra attention, or should it be credited to the method? Other questions arise: Is the improvement a lasting or merely a temporary one? Are the groups really comparable? Were not the test students more highly motivated, since they knew they were being tested and wanted the test to succeed? It would be difficult to devise the equivalent of a placebo, but is not one required in these situations? These are some of the many doubts and questionings that assail those whose task it is to interpret the findings and to reach a decision as to how effective the method is and whether it should be recommended for adoption.

From these four examples it is now possible to understand some of the reasons why the experimental method as applied to human beings has not gained the ready acceptance and use it enjoys in the physical sciences. Its shortcomings are real as applied to the problems of people, and this is one reason why social science has lagged so far behind physical science. Clearly a different method is required.

Up to this point, the examples of experiments have dealt with a world that is completely familiar to the layman. The subjects in these experiments have been metals, animals, hospitalized heart patients, and junior high school students. It is possible for the typical person to think concretely about each test—who was involved, what was involved. A new procedure, now being developed, is based entirely on the sampling process and the laws of probability, both of which lead the untutored layman into an unreal world that is difficult for him to comprehend.

Moreover, the new procedure meets with another kind of resistance from an unusual source. Often it appears to deny the individual's own personal experience and the philosophy he has evolved on the basis of that experience. The life each individual lives constantly impresses him with his own uniqueness. He is truly different from every other person in the world, past and present. His tastes are different, his habits are different, his philosophy is different, and his physical appearance is different.

Yet his uniqueness is due solely to chance, and chance enters into every aspect of his daily life. His birth and race and religion are largely products of chance. He may be injured or killed by an automobile any day. His house may catch on fire. He may have a sudden heart attack. He may find himself in an occupation for which he had not planned. Even his marriage may come about largely by chance. In short, he is a creature of chance, and this uncertainty colors his whole point of view.

As an individual, his existence is as unpredictable as that of any particle of matter that goes bouncing about in its microcosm in a completely random manner. It is only when the number of individuals and the number of particles have reached a given size that individuals taken together, or particles taken together, begin to behave in predictable ways and according to a pattern. Chance, which at the individual level is all important, is constantly reduced as numbers increase, and the uniqueness of the individual no longer has any real significance in the world of large numbers.

Professor Mario Salvadori of Columbia states the case in this fashion: "It would be wonderful to know exactly how one man or one nucleus will behave under certain circumstances, but since, in general, we have to deal with a large number of men and of nuclei, we can be at least partially satisfied with some kind of average knowledge or knowledge of the average. Here the language of probability comes to our help. It is impossible to say today who will be crossing 42nd Street at Fifth Avenue in New York tomorrow at 10 A.M. but it is easy to predict how many people will do so."

Some years ago Arthur Conan Doyle put these words, borrowed from an earlier writer, into the mouth of one of his characters: "While the individual man is an insoluble puzzle, in the aggregate he becomes a mathematical certainty. You can never foretell what any one man will do, but you can say with precision what an average number will be up to. Individuals vary, but averages remain constant."

This statement, most students will agree, is too far-reaching as to the certainties of large numbers, but it does point to a very basic truth and to the very great possibilities for research on social problems based upon large numbers.

Proof of this can be seen on all hands. Life insurance companies cannot possibly identify those policy holders who will die during the coming years, but they can, with great accuracy, predict the *total number* of policy holders who will. By the same token, fire insurance companies cannot identify the houses that will catch fire during the next few months, but they can arrive at a highly accurate estimate of the total number of fires and the likely losses.

The same laws of probability applied to large numbers operate in every field; and were this not the case, the whole world, physical and social, would be thrown into an unbelievable state of chaos.

A New Method for Solving Old Problems

Traditionally, the scientific method has consisted of systematic observation and experimentation. During the last century, and more particularly during recent decades, sampling methods and statistical analyses have enjoyed growing use as the value of these mathematical tools has come to be better understood and appreciated.

Statistical methods have been important in the growth of the social sciences. The physical sciences, likewise, have found them to be of increasing importance. Statistical analysis, in fact, is useful in virtually all types of scientific investigation. Because certain truths can be arrived at only through the statistical approach—without benefit of observation or experimentation unless the definition of these is tortured—a good case can be made for adding statistical analysis to the two traditional methods of science.

A whole new order of scientific knowledge is possible through the statistical analysis of mass experience. Even the social scientists have been slow to recognize the exciting possibilities this procedure offers in dealing with many of the knottiest social problems of the day. A start has hardly been made in the use of this new method.

The word *new* as it is used here needs to be correctly understood. In a sense, nothing is new; somewhere and at some time some person has had the same idea. Bacon did not invent the experimental method or inductive reasoning; their earliest use undoubtedly antedates history. His great contribution was to focus attention on them in a manner forceful enough to establish them in the minds of men as fruitful ways of discovering new knowledge about the physical world.

The difference between the experimental approach and the statistical approach can be illustrated by the controversy that has erupted over the relationship between cigarette smoking and lung cancer. The scientist who is wed to the experimental method has refused to admit that a causal connection exists, since it has been impossible up to this time to isolate a virus or some other cancer-causing factor in the laboratory and to induce the disease in human tissue. Until this has been accomplished, he is prone to assert that scientific proof of any relationship is lacking.

On the other hand, the scientist who believes in statistical analysis as a way of arriving at scientific truth insists that the statistical evidence does prove a causal relationship. He can show that those who smoke cigarettes are far more likely to be afflicted with lung cancer than non-smokers and by odds that are far greater than pure chance. He can also show that heavy smokers are much more likely to develop lung cancer than light smokers, and that light smokers, in turn, are far more likely to be afflicted than non-smokers.

The laboratory scientist may say that this relationship is spurious, that it is merely coincidental, and that smoking is not the necessary cause. The public is caught in the middle. However, in most situations people are more inclined to accept clinical proof than statistical proof, largely because they are less familiar with the latter. The truth is that one method is exactly as scientific as the other; both rest upon the laws of probability, as does all science.

The first interest of the researcher in dealing with a situation of this character is to see if a relationship can be established by the simple process of finding out whether two factors accompany each other in a time sequence. Do more smokers get lung cancer than non-smokers? Do enough more get lung cancer to rule out pure chance? The next step, typically, is to follow a rule set out by Bacon, which in this case requires the researcher to determine whether the increased use of cigarettes is accompanied by the increased incidence of cancer. If the heavy smokers were no more likely to get lung cancer than the light smokers, the relationship might seriously be questioned.

To establish a statistical relationship is important, but it is not enough. Through the application of statistical methods to mass experience it is possible to investigate many facets of a problem. In the case of lung cancer this approach can reveal what types of smokers (physical and psychological) are more likely to be afflicted and which environmental factors seem to be related. (It has already been shown that people living in rural areas are less susceptible.) What part does inheritance play? What are the working and living habits of those who do get lung cancer as opposed to those who smoke similar amounts but *do not get it?*

The great insights that can be obtained from the statistical approach to mass experience will be illustrated later by research that has attempted to follow this plan.

Health, Happiness, and Long Life

Scientific methods now widely used have left unexplored many of the important aspects of life. The reason is that these methods do not lend themselves easily to the study of people and to environmental factors, which have an important influence on people. This is why the new procedure will fill a vital need.

Three experiments will help to illustrate the point by showing how the new research has been employed to shed light on three of man's most important concerns: health, happiness, and long life.

Health, of course, has been the object of research throughout the centuries, and particularly during the last sixty years. The great advances made in conquering disease have been brought about largely by clinical research and laboratory experimentation, as well as by expanding knowledge in all fields of science. At the same time, there has been surprisingly little attention given to environmental factors, which have an important impact upon health and often contribute to or aggravate illness.

Until recent years there has not been a scientific study of the factors and conditions that make for happiness, although happiness has been man's dream from the time he acquired the mantle of *Homo sapiens*.

Even before Hippocrates, men were beginning to speculate on long life and how to attain it; but little has been done by science to find out the reasons certain persons live to a ripe old age. The reason, again, is that laboratory methods are not suitable for finding answers to health problems when environmental factors play an important part.

Therefore, there is need for a new method especially suited to deal with people in their social environment. In the pages that follow, three studies will be described that have been made largely by the statistical approach.

It should also be borne in mind that they were not costly studies involving hundreds of thousands of dollars. When the modest sums required are compared with the hundreds of millions now being spent in laboratory research on health problems, one can see how much can be learned by the new method at small expenditure.

How the New Procedure Was Used to Shed Light on a Disease

Infantile paralysis is a disease that probably goes back to earliest times. Many instances of paralysis mentioned in the Bible are probably due to this ailment. Infantile paralysis was first described by a London doctor by the name of Michael Underwood in the year 1789. Over the next 160 years following the first treatise on this disease more than ten thousand studies and reports were of sufficient importance to be included in a bibliography on the disease.

Fortunately the virus that causes polio was eventually isolated in the laboratory, and Dr. Jonas Salk discovered that the killed bacteria could be safely and effectively used in a vaccine to prevent the disease. Later Dr. Albert Sabin found that children and adults could be inoculated with a weak live strain to produce the same immunization. As a result, infantile paralysis, which was one of the most dread diseases of mankind, has been virtually conquered—just as smallpox, diphtheria, typhus, yellow fever, and other contagious diseases were conquered in earlier times by the same process of isolating the virus, then immunizing the public with a vaccine made from the killed or attenuated bacteria.

In the not too distant future all contagious and infectious diseases are likely to be brought under control by the same type of medical research. In fact, the list of those still to be conquered grows shorter every year.

Medical research can now turn more and more to the ailments of man that are not bacteria-borne. Inevitably this research must concern itself with environmental factors—as opposed to biological and physiological factors. Take the case of heart disease. New types of operations and drugs are helping the victims of heart disease; but there has been little attention to the environmental factors that induce it. J. N. Morris, writing in the *Listener* on the subject of coronary thrombosis, made this interesting comment: "Among non-medical people I meet, there is a widely prevalent idea that research into the possible connections between diseases like coronary thrombosis and the way people live is a leading activity of modern medicine. The idea is wrong. Many of the London Teaching Hospitals, for example, give little support to investigations such as I have been describing, and there are great provincial schools where the record is similar. This is undoubtedly one of the reasons for the slow progress being made in preventive medicine, and for its prevalent pessimism, compared with the massive achievements and faith in the future of the clinical branches. This situation is not accidental; the causes lie deep in the social and academic structure of medicine and its recent intellectual history—particularly its highly successful struggle to become more scientific through laboratory experiment."

The study of poliomyelitis described here was undertaken to discover factors associated with susceptibility to this ailment, or to put it more simply, to find out if certain living conditions, psychological factors, and health factors—which could not be adequately studied in the laboratory—had some connection with polio. The study was completed just prior to the introduction of the Salk vaccine and is therefore of interest only in illustrating how a statistical approach can bring to light certain factors that the medical profession and the medical researchers working on this disease could not have, or at least had not, discovered.

Mostly out of curiosity to see if such a procedure, discussed earlier, could be useful in developing leads that other medical researchers could pursue, the writer went to Basil O'Connor, head of the National Foundation for Infantile Paralysis, with the proposal to make a study of this type. No person, it should be added, has so persistently and intelligently conducted a search to conquer any disease as he, and no one is so deserving of credit for the great success that was brought about eventually as a result of the forces he marshalled through many years. He was willing to try anything that offered the slightest hope of shedding light on the disease he set out to conquer.

It is no secret that the medical profession frowns upon any kind of research that is not undertaken by doctors and is not conducted in strictly orthodox ways. For this reason, no one in the medical profession was apprised of the study.

The survey employed, probably for the first time in a medical study, a nationwide control group. A representative sample of victims of polio in the 1950 epidemic was carefully selected by approved methods. Each case was then "matched," or paired by age, sex, and race, with an individual living in the same community who had not contracted the disease. For example, if a girl, age thirteen, in Hopewell, New Jersey, had suffered an attack during that epidemic, another girl of the same age, same race, and same socio-economic status in Hopewell, who had not contracted the disease, was paired with the victim.

Interviews were distributed by approved methods in all sections of the country and paralleled closely the distribution of cases affected by polio in that year. The interview itself embraced more than three hundred items and required, on the average, two to four hours of interviewing time. A total of 1,067 polio victims made up the patient group, and a similar number the control group.

Many hypotheses were explored. Some had been advanced by medical researchers in this field; others came from volunteer workers for the National Foundation. Still others came from laymen. Any idea as to the cause of polio or the factors related to susceptibility to it was given consideration. Some of them were extraordinarily bizarre. One volunteer worker said that she had noted that children often got polio where new plastering was being done. Another said she thought polio was due to a salt deficiency. Others said that the presence on the lawn of a willow tree was likely to give a child polio. Still others had theories about streams, swimming pools, nearness to horse barns, and dozens of similar ideas; in fact, more than one hundred different suggestions were considered. The final interviewing form that was used included many of these strange ideas; but it also included many facts pertaining to possible exposure, housing and living conditions, eating and sleeping habits, psychological factors, and a fairly extensive medical history of each person and his parents.

From a study of this type many thousands of facts can be developed when the data are analyzed and "cross tabulations" are made between results to different questions. In the instances in which the results between patient and control groups are great enough to rule out chance factors, the findings become statistically significant and can then be examined from the point of view of possible causal relationship.

The term "statistically significant" is one with which readers should be familiar, if they are not already. In the case of tonsillectomies, the results do not "prove" that a person who has never had his tonsils removed will not get polio, nor that those who have had them removed will. It simply means that the chances are greater that those who have tonsillectomies will be susceptible than those who have not. Many factors, or a combination of many factors, are nearly always present in the case of those who fall victim to a disease.

What, then, did this new approach yield that was not already established by orthodox procedures? First, the findings helped settle a long-standing argument within the medical profession. The results clearly indicated that persons who had had their tonsils removed at any time in their life were more susceptible. Up to this point it had been thought that tonsillectomies should not be performed during a polio epidemic, but even this view was disputed by many doctors. Three years later, the relationship was definitely established between polio and tonsillectomies by medical researchers and is now generally accepted.

One of the theories advanced by a volunteer worker, Miss Ruth Kissel, of Somerset County, New Jersey, was that polio victims gave evidence of a salt deficiency in their diets. The study bore out Miss Kissel's hypothesis. Since salt loss is greatest in the hottest months, this may be one of the many reasons why the number of cases tends to reach a peak at the end of the summer months.

After this study was completed, a team of medical researchers in England, working in the county of Essex, found that the incidence of polio tended to vary with the salinity of the water, which in the case of this county comes from three different sources. In those communities where the water had the greatest salinity, the number of polio cases was less than in those areas where there was less salt in the drinking water.

It is difficult to probe objectively into psychological factors, but it is well established that they have a predisposing influence in the case of many ailments. In this study an attempt was made for the first time to discover whether certain personality types were more susceptible to polio than others. The results indicated that a significantly higher proportion of parents of polio victims described their children in such terms as "nervous," "fidgety," "high-strung," as compared to the number who described them as "easy," "relaxed," and the like. Further evidence that psychological factors are involved came from ascertainable facts regarding the victim's home life. A higher incidence of the disease, for example, was found in the homes where there had been divorces. More stricken homes had had recent deaths in the family; more had suffered mental shocks, crises, or great disappointments.

One of the more interesting findings of the study fell in line with an earlier discovery by two investigators, Litman and Bosma, in the Minnesota epidemic of 1946. These two researchers found that children who contracted polio had, as a group, not shown the same satisfactory growth pattern as their classmates or, in fact, as their own brothers and sisters. The differences were great enough between the two groups to rule out chance factors.

In the case of the study reported here, a similar finding was revealed. In the case of boys under ten years of age, 40% of the patient group had not gained weight during the year preceding the attack, or had actually lost weight. In the control group, only half this number had not gained, or had lost weight, during the same period. The same relationship was found to exist between the age groups of ten years through nineteen, although in the case of girls the differences were less marked.

Many early findings of medical researchers were confirmed. It had long been known that strenuous physical exercise usually precedes the onslaught of the disease. In approximately half of all the cases investigated, the person affected had engaged in more than normal physical activity in the days prior to the attack and, as a result, had been more than normally fatigued.

The National Foundation had warned parents not to take children on trips during an epidemic. Evidence as to the correctness of this advice was found in the survey. Of the polio victims more than four in ten had been away from home for at least one night during the month previous to the attack.

Strangely, it was found that more children who were afflicted had lived in their present dwelling less than a year than was true of the control group. This finding reveals one of the interesting ways in which theories evolve and why, without further investigation, they may lead to wrong conclusions. It will be recalled that one volunteer worker said that it was her observation that children were likely to get polio in homes where plastering was being done. It was obviously not the plaster that was related to polio, but more likely that the children living in these houses probably were moving into them for the first time—into a new neighborhood where they were exposed to a possibly different strain of the virus—with all of the psychological factors that are present when children move into new and strange neighborhoods.

Equally revealing were the many theories disproved by this particular approach. Bottle-fed infants were no more susceptible than breast-fed babies. No evidence was found that inoculations or immunizations predisposed a child to polio. There seemed to be no connection with allergies, or with eye, ear, or nose troubles. Both groups had about the same medical histories with respect to childhood diseases. First-born children were found to be no more likely to get polio than later-born children. Children in both groups had the same weight at birth, and the same number were full term and not premature. They came from the same kind of homes. No difference was found by income or occupation. Children in poor families were no more likely to get polio than those in rich homes. There was no difference found by type of dwelling or the number of persons living in the home. These are but a few of the many hypotheses ruled out by the findings.

What place will this type of procedure occupy in medical research in the future? Certainly the new method will never replace the type of laboratory research that has been so successful in the past. On the other hand, the statistical approach will be given more and more attention because of its usefulness in exploring factors, chiefly environmental, that are all but impossible to investigate by orthodox experimental methods, and which will assume greater importance as the degenerative diseases become the focus of interest. Statistical analysis is especially well suited to produce leads and to sort out the many influences having to do with the way people live, which are related to human ailments.

Factors Contributing to Long Life

Since early Greek days Western man has speculated about the reasons for long life. He has always hoped that someone will find a magic water, a special food or diet, a root or a pill, which will prolong life; whatever it is must be quick and easy, something that will not disturb his accustomed way of life.

When a fortunate individual reaches the age of one hundred, he has the journalistic right to have a feature article in the newspapers, in which he is given the chance to tell the world how he reached this ripe old age. His views usually cover a narrow range of causes: he never touched a drop of liquor in his life, or he took a drink every day; he never used tobacco, or he was an inveterate smoker; he worked hard, or he took every possible chance to relax. If to this confusion of conflicting theories is added the misinterpretation of mortality figures and the lack of accurate record-keeping in most countries, some conception can be gained of the difficulties of conducting meaningful research on the factors contributing to long life.

One of the great achievements of science in modern times has been to prolong life. Within the present century life expectancy has been increased by more than twenty years. Unfortunately, the layman is prone to misinterpret these figures. The increase in life expectancy is largely due to the dramatic decrease in infant mortality and the great decline in childhood diseases. Life expectancy for those who reach the age of sixty is not markedly greater today than it was a hundred years ago. One of the reasons, of course, is that many who are physically unfit and who in other times would have died early in life survive to the age of sixty and over. Even so, it can be said that laboratory and clinical methods have not contributed much to man's life after sixty, nor have they contributed much in the way of understanding the problems of achieving a long life.

Any investigation of persons who have reached the very old age of ninety and over must take full account of the tendency to exaggerate, or to forget, just how old one is. Census enumerators must record the age as given to them; consequently, they are at the mercy of those who have no definite idea or proof, and census data for this group are usually erroneous. Adequate birth records are maintained in very few nations, either by the state or by the church. Moreover, another phenomenon is found in countries of high illiteracy. The number of persons who claim to be one hundred years old, or older, tends to increase with the extent of illiteracy. Where people cannot read—or count—they are tempted to add a few years to their age when they get to be old enough to boast about it.

Life expectancy figures provide a good guide to the probable number of persons who are near the age of one hundred. In northern European nations life expectancy is greater than it is in Great Britain or the United States. The Western nations as a group are far ahead of the rest of the world, where health standards are lower. It is chiefly for these reasons that one should be suspicious of the claims made by countries of the Middle East and South America as to the great number of their centenarians.

Environmental factors obviously have much to do with longevity, and this is why the statistical approach is well suited to study this particular problem. The method is particularly useful when a condition or situation results from many factors and not just a few. In the case of long life, not only living habits and conditions are involved but also many biological and psychological factors.

With the purpose of seeing what could be learned about old age by the method described in earlier pages, a study was designed to embrace a representative nationwide sample of persons who had reached the age of ninety-five and over—in both the United States and Great Britain. The latter country was added to see if differences that exist in living habits between the United States and Great Britain have any measurable influence on longevity. In a sense, the older persons interviewed in Great Britain constituted a control group.

A total of 530 persons were interviewed in the two nations. Of these, 193 were one hundred years of age or older. The oldest person included claimed to be 116 years old. The interview required some three hours on the average and covered more than two hundred items having to do with diet, ancestry, physical characteristics, psychological attitudes, occupational record, health history, sleeping, drinking, smoking habits, and many other aspects of the person's life. Memories often become hazy at this age, and so, whenever feasible, information was checked with other members of the family. Approximately twice as many women as men live to be ninety-five and over; and they were included in this study in approximately this ratio.

Full details of the investigation of these nonagenarians and centenarians were published in the *Saturday Evening Post*, which sponsored the study, and in a book entitled *Secrets of Long Life*. Some of the salient facts can be summarized briefly here, and their implications for society pointed out.

One of the advantages of this type of approach, it should be noted, is to discover which of the many widely held theories are borne out by statistical evidence, and to provide a basis for appraising their importance. The investigator hopes to find factors that have been overlooked, or underestimated in their importance, and to affirm or deny those that have come to be regarded as fully established.

The importance of heredity has been widely accepted. Dr. Oliver Wendell Holmes once recommended that people who wished to live to an advanced age should "advertise for a couple of parents, both belonging to long-lived families, some years before birth." The findings of this study bear out the importance of heredity. At the same time, they show that too much importance may have been placed upon this factor. Fully half of the oldsters investigated had parents who did not live to the age of eighty; in fact, one in four had neither parent, sister, nor brother who lived to the age of eighty.

As early as the time of Hippocrates it was observed that fat persons seldom live to an advanced age. This observation, and the generally held view that overweight predisposes one to many ailments that terminate life at a relatively early age, are fully substantiated by the study. The men investigated weighed approximately fifteen pounds less at the age of thirty and fifty than the average man of that age today in the United States. Even when height was considered, and the fact that today's adult males are approximately two inches taller than those of three generations ago, the weight of the men included in the study was still on the low side. The difference is far less marked in the case of women; in fact, when height was taken into account, the weight figures of the women at different intervals in their life approximated the average.

Much has been written about food and its effect upon long life. Food faddists are numerous, and their arguments sound entirely plausible: we are what we eat. But food cults will find small comfort in the findings of this investigation. With very few exceptions, the men and women of ninety-five years and older ate what they described in their own words as "plain cooking," and a careful check of their food preferences would certainly indicate as much. In many instances the food, and the way it was prepared, would shock any modern dietitian. They were not "choosy," and they certainly were not gourmets. Only a tiny number were vegetarians or had ever followed any special diet of any type.

While the food eaten by these older persons throughout their lives was of the most ordinary and general sort, and was prepared in the manner of housewives who are not too much concerned with quality, there is one major and all-important fact about their food habits: they were light eaters. They ate only at meal times, and usually only one helping then. Typically they ate no snacks between meals and nothing at bedtime. Most said that they ate less than those who lived with them—most of whom had long since departed this world. From this part of the investigation the conclusion seems warranted that what one eats is relatively less important than the amount consumed.

Analysis of the data regarding other living habits—sleeping, smoking, drinking, relaxation, and the like—indicates that these older persons, as a group, lived up to the Greek injunction: all things in moderation. Most followed a regular daily pattern of early to bed and early to rise. Many of them smoked tobacco in one form or another most of their lives, and many consumed alcoholic beverages—but almost always in moderate amounts. The cigarette smokers generally quit smoking in their later years, or turned to cigars and pipes.

Very few could at any time in their lives be described as "hell raisers," and if the study had embraced only this aspect of their lives, the conclusion would be inescapable that, as a group, they lived an unexciting existence.

One of the most significant findings of the investigation is the importance of physical activity in attaining a very old age. At the time that these men and women reached adulthood—about 1880—farming was the chief occupation of the country and the number of manual workers was high. The number engaged in business and professional pursuits was correspondingly low. The hours worked each week, by present-day standards, were extraordinarily long. They left school at an early age (the seventh or eighth grade on the average) and went to work. They retired long after the accepted retiring age of sixty-five today. Only half ever took a vacation during all their working years. In fact, when the total number of hours worked is computed for an entire lifetime, the amazing fact emerges that the typical man in this group actually worked as many hours as two men would in this day and age.

Persons in sedentary jobs do not survive as long as those who engage in physical activity and who are on their feet most of the day. It may be this very fact that accounts for the greater longevity of women compared to men. Women are busy most of the day performing household chores; and while their work may not be so strenuous as that of some males, still the typical housewife is jumping about all day long, taking charge of the children, feeding the family, doing the cleaning, and performing the other tasks about the home. It is a rare woman who can remain seated most of the day—and certainly few were found who had spent their lives this way.

Apart from the many years most of these very old persons carried on some type of physical activity, the other important respect in which they differ from the great mass of their fellow men is in their attitudes toward life. As a group they lived happy, contented lives. They worried little, preferring to take life as it came. They were easy-going, and did not fret because they did not have more education or because they did not have more money. They found pleasure in simple things. They enjoyed their friends, got along well with their wives, their families, and relatives, and liked their communities and their way of life.

In short, these older persons were uncomplicated, well-adjusted persons, who took life as it came without fretting or worrying. One of the reasons they lived so long is the obvious one that they enjoyed life—they liked living. They always had something to do, and they retained their interest in what was going on in the world. Most of those interviewed were found to be surprisingly alert; despite poor eyesight and other physical disabilities, many read daily newspapers and magazines with as much interest as those a half-century younger.

While this study has served to provide another example of the type of problem that lends itself to the analysis of mass experience —as opposed to the experimental approach—there are important implications in it for the future of man. Intellectual vigor undoubtedly is related to physical vigor; and it is probably no mere coincidence that the Greeks gave so much attention to physical prowess in the period of their greatest intellectual triumphs.

The progress of man has all but done away with hard physical work. Some way must be found to remedy this situation, even if it means blocking off whole streets in our cities and towns for those who wish to walk.

The importance of keeping weight within reasonable bounds is fully recognized and, in fact, is responsible for the special diet crazes that perennially sweep the country. What has not been generally recognized is the fact that the habit of eating three "square" meals a day is pretty much an American custom, which goes back to the time when most men arose before six o'clock in the morning, did the chores before breakfast, and then worked in the fields until dark. The practice, which started in America's pioneering days, still is carried on in a time when the habits of life—and of work—have changed completely. Perhaps the time has come to follow the custom of most countries and have only one substantial meal a day. Certainly the needs of the body could be fully met with only this amount of food.

Factors Relating to Happiness

The third example, illustrating how statistical procedures can be applied to problems which the methods of observation and experimentation have left untouched, deals with the broad and nebulous subject of happiness. Difficult to define, happiness is the very kind of problem the new methodology can explore and illuminate.

Happiness has been a goal of most men throughout time and an object of much speculation. One might think, therefore, that through the ages happiness would have been the subject of many systematic studies; but this has not been the case. In fact, almost no attention has been devoted to it by scholars and scientists. The entire literature on the subject would not fill one library shelf; by way of contrast, the number of books on religion would fill a whole wing of a very large library.

Neat definitions are not possible or even necessary in studying happiness. Virtually every one has an idea of what happiness means to him, and in terms of his own definition can give a reasonably accurate estimate of how happy he is. Studies made in recent years have indicated the reliability and the validity of people's own judgments about themselves. These self-ratings agree well with the expert judgments of clinicians who have closely observed small groups of persons.

Important work on the fears and aspirations of the people of

182

different nations of the world is now being carried on by Dr. Hadley Cantril, head of the Institute for International Social Research and former head of the department of psychology of Princeton University. Dr. Cantril has developed a type of scale that can be used with persons of all levels of education for the purpose of discovering what their goals in life are, and the extent to which they are achieving these goals. Meaningful comparisons can be made between one nation and another; and the employment of the scales in both the more advanced and the underdeveloped areas of the world should reveal much about people in this present era of rapid social change and political evolution.

Other investigations of happiness that are now being made, or have been undertaken on a pilot basis in the past, have sought to explore the many factors that seem to be related to happiness. Studies of limited scope have been made in the United States, France, Canada, Great Britain, and the Netherlands. Although of a tentative and exploratory character, these studies have brought to light many interesting facts.

It will come as no surprise that in the United States family, jobs, friends, and health play an important role in happiness; the degree or extent of their importance, however, may be surprising. The individual who can honestly say that he gets on well with his wife and family, is satisfied with his job and his circle of friends, and enjoys reasonably good health is almost certain to fall close to the "very happy" end of the spectrum. If he has to answer No to any of these questions, his chances are reduced accordingly.

Many things that seem to be important as conditions of happiness turn out to be relatively unimportant. For example, most citizens of the United States think they would be happier if they had more money. The findings indicate that once a certain minimum amount is passed, money makes rather little difference. Likewise, most adults in the United States believe they would be happier if they had more education. But again, above a certain minimum level, education does not make much difference. Even age seems to make little difference. Younger people are inclined to think they will be happier at a later period of their life; older people are prone to think they were happier at some earlier period.

When the persons who can properly be described as happy are compared with those in the unhappy category, a rather marked difference in outlook on life is discovered. Unhappy people tend to put the blame for their unhappiness upon circumstances and things they cannot help—more than upon themselves and traits of character.

Happy people, compared with the unhappy people, tend to follow a different pattern in their leisure-time habits. Those who are happy tend to find pleasure in reading, gardening, and the quiet diversions. Unhappy persons, on the contrary, tend to look for excitement in movies, television, parties, drinking, and similar forms of entertainment and escape. The happy people are likely to be religious and, in their opinion, to get much help from their religious beliefs.

Persons living in smaller communities apparently get more enjoyment out of life than those who live in larger communities, particularly those who live in the largest metropolitan centers. As might be expected, business and professional people get more pleasure out of their work and tend to be happier than those who work at manual labor. The least happy persons found in the United States are those who work in factories at manual and repetitive tasks and live in the largest cities.

One of the more interesting findings of the studies that have been made is that people in the United States who live in sight of mountains seem to be happier than those who live in the plains states. Whether there is any causal relationship between happiness and the character of the landscape must obviously be established by further research. However, this does serve to illustrate the kind of insight that is possible from the application of the new research procedure to problems that have been neglected in the past.

The concept of happiness varies from country to country; the degree of happiness enjoyed by the people of any one country varies from time to time. Soon after World War II the people of France,

Holland, and Canada were disposed to identify happiness with financial security to a much greater extent than was true of the United States and Great Britain. This was especially true of France, where the greatest proportion of unhappy to happy persons was found. It is also significant that in France, at that time, a very high percentage of those who supported Communist candidates rated themselves as unhappy.

Knowledge about the factors related to happiness should be useful to present and future generations. In fact, it is not inconceivable that the philosophy of a nation might undergo an appreciable change over a period of time if it could be definitely established by scientific procedures that the possession of wealth did not necessarily bring happiness. The mad pursuit for money might then lose some of its driving force. People with a materialistic philosophy might be led in time to look for happiness within the mind, and not in material possessions.

Better knowledge about the fears and hopes of people in all parts of the world should help to guide those governments that have assumed the responsibility for providing financial and other types of aid, particularly in the case of the underdeveloped nations. Moreover, an understanding about the destiny of people of the world, as the people themselves see it, should be of inestimable value in working out a lasting peace.

Problems That Computers Can
Help to Solve

The electronic computer is an invaluable aid to the new kind of research described in the preceding pages. It can store great quantities of data, deal with many variables, and make possible analyses of many kinds. The same statistical operations would require an army of trained personnel working months or even years to duplicate.

Because of the speed of their operation and the relatively low cost entailed, many useful projects become possible, which otherwise might not be undertaken because of the great amount of money required. One of many such projects that could be listed and that should help to advance medical science is a computer center maintained by the medical profession for the purpose of processing case histories collected throughout the country.

One of the rituals of medical practice is to obtain a case history of each person who enters a hospital as a patient. Millions of hours are spent in gathering such data from the millions of patients with every known affliction. The purpose is commendable, and it is this fact gathering that has been so important in the progress of medical science. While the idea is sound, the truth is that very little use is made of the vast amount of information collected. Typically, these case histories go into the files, where they are available for any medical researcher who has any particular interest in them, but mostly they merely gather dust.

The medical profession could, if it so desired, establish a national computer center where copies of these case histories, placed upon standardized forms, would be sent. The form would contain complete information about the patient; it would also contain a detailed account of the treatment, and the facts about his recovery rate. At the computer center all this information would be transferred to tapes, stored, and analyzed.

Many medical practices, widely followed by the profession today, could and should be subjected to careful scrutiny. The medical profession has the same tendency to hold on to practices, once they are widely accepted, as those engaged in other pursuits. For example, it was only two decades ago that most hospitals gave up the practice of giving purgatives indiscriminately to patients on entering. This practice was not only useless but actually harmful in some cases.

Another important medical discovery had to await chance and the accidents of war. This is early ambulation. Lack of hospital beds in treating the battlefield wounded made it necessary to get surgical patients out of bed as soon as possible—a practice that proved so successful in their recovery that it has become routine in hospitals today.

The great question mark is the number of medical practices still followed today that time will show to be equally useless and harmful. With the help of computers and the vast amount of data that is already being collected, all medical practices should be examined constantly.

Doctors could have available for their guidance the analyzed data from thousands of cases, not just the few drawn from their own experience or the necessarily limited numbers reported upon in the medical journals. Machines will never replace human judgment. At the same time, it must be remembered that judgment is based largely upon facts and experience.

With electronic computers many new facts can be brought to light, which laboratory and clinical research are unable to provide. The subtle relationship between diseases and the multiple symptoms that are often encountered can be examined meaningfully only when thousands of cases are taken into account and when those that fit into a special category are sufficient in number to warrant reliable findings. A medical computing center would be equipped to deal with these relationships, and out of it should come a whole new order of medical discoveries.

Industrial Disease

Another example of how computers can help solve problems that now confront society concerns the chronic disease of modern industrial society—unemployment. In fact, much more progress could be made in dealing with this particular problem if it were generally regarded as a disease. If unemployment were regarded in the same light as a highly contagious ailment, then almost certainly it would be dealt with in a vigorous manner. Outbreaks would be carefully and quickly pinpointed, and facts of many kinds collected regarding those who had become unemployed, the nature of the work they were doing, the community, and the industry itself.

The causes of unemployment are manifold, and this is why corrective measures cannot be taken intelligently in the absence of detailed and current information. Without this knowledge, those who are required to make decisions are forced to operate as blindly as would medical practitioners if they had to prescribe for patients without careful examination.

The establishment of a government center to deal with this problem could be accomplished for a relatively small outlay of money. It could provide detailed information, properly analyzed, for the guidance of the public, legislators, and government administrators.

Such a plan would require that each unemployed person appear once a week, at his local post office, to fill out a standard form containing the necessary information about himself and the character of his employment. To fill out such a form once a week might, on occasion, be inconvenient—but not any more so than the very many forms that employers are now required by law to fill out.

After these forms were received at the computing center and the information contained in them recorded by the machines, detailed reports for every community of the nation would be possible in a matter of a few days. In many instances the community itself, having complete and up-to-date information about the condition of unemployment, could institute corrective measures without waiting for federal or state action. Certainly such information would help the community to plan its spending for public projects on a more informed basis.

Presently unemployment data are collected by monthly samplings. These are extremely useful, and because they are done by the best cross-section methods, they are highly accurate. They cannot, unfortunately, provide the detailed information required for each community. Nor are the samples large enough to provide data for small segments of the population.

To gain a better understanding of the value of information collected on a national basis and analyzed by computers, the following examples are offered. In a certain city a steady rise has been registered in the number of unemployed young adults who were engaged in bookkeeping jobs in small industries. These young men, the computer analysis reveals, had high school courses in bookkeeping, and their loss of jobs is due largely to the introduction of new electronic bookkeeping methods. Since bookkeeping jobs are almost certain to decline in the years ahead, two corrective steps are indicated for immediate action: the high schools in the city need to be alerted to the lessening demand for this type of employee; and the young men who are out of work need to be retrained quickly for other types of work.

In another area, it is discovered that the number of unemployed is increasing among salesmen whose jobs are to call upon small retail grocery outlets. The analysis shows that these men, especially those over the age of forty-five, are having difficulty finding employment in this field. The same problem arose earlier in another area of the country, and it was brought to light through the computer analysis that many men who formerly had been employed in this work had found that they could shift to the field of insurance. However, those who made the transition with success were the ones who spent a minimum of three months in training programs conducted by the insurance companies.

The above examples are cited mostly to show the kind of detailed information that could be provided by computer methods and its usefulness in helping local authorities to take corrective measures.

The amount of money that would have to be appropriated by the government to maintain such a center would not be inconsiderable; but in terms of lost wages it would be small. If it is assumed that the average income of the group of unemployed persons of the nation is about $60 a week, then the five to six million unemployed lose a total of $300,000,000 a week. Certainly a center could be operated for a year on far less than the amount lost each week in wages.

Increasing specialization creates its own problems and makes more vital the establishment of an intelligence system that can quickly alert the public and educators to the changing needs of business, industry, and the professions. The great financial loss to the individuals involved in unemployment, and to society, can be roughly calculated in terms of lost wages. However, the even greater loss to human dignity and to family relations can only be surmised. Multiple evils follow in the wake of unemployment—alcoholism, crime and delinquency, broken homes. Society can no longer afford to think of unemployment as an act of Providence or as a shortcoming that is inherent in the free enterprise system. Unemployment must be dealt with as any serious disease—and it cannot be dealt with intelligently as such without a lot more facts than are now available.

PART V

ACCELERATING CHANGE

Change and the Future

The thinking of civilized man has always been oriented to the past. He studies history to understand the present and to predict the future—but his thinking seldom reaches that far. In a very real sense he backs into the future; he most certainly does not face it.

Looking backward over the last few hundred years, man marvels at his great achievements. It almost never occurs to him that just as much progress, and perhaps even more, can and will be made during the coming centuries. Since this is obviously true, his objective should be to anticipate the changes ahead, then attempt to attain in decades goals that might otherwise require centuries.

The judgment of the world a thousand years hence may be that Western man is still living in or emerging from the Middle Ages. However this may be, it should be reasonably clear that the speed of transition to the next higher level of civilization will depend to a great extent upon man's acceptance of change. A careful examination of man's attitude toward change is therefore needed to gain some insight into the reasons why he so often resists it.

It will be helpful to point out that man clings tenaciously to the *status quo* in some areas of life and not in others. He does not resist change per se. He may only shrug his shoulders in helplessness when he contemplates the failures in his political system, while at the same time eagerly seeking change in his standard of living. He accepts new drugs and new medical practices even before their effectiveness has been established. He purchases new products for his home with the conviction that if they are new, they must be better. In fact, the most powerful word that can be employed in advertising, at least in the United States, is the word *new*. The progress that he so earnestly seeks is the progress associated with the invention and improvement of material things; unfortunately it is not the progress associated with the invention and improvement of political and social forms and practices.

Resistance to change, upon further analysis, generally falls into four broad categories. The first has to do with resistance that arises out of the confusion between ends and means. The goals of any society remain fairly constant over long periods of time. Means must be changed constantly to attain these constant goals.

To the politically naïve, almost any change in the practices or means of government is likely to become confused with the goals of government. For this reason, even the most needed and obvious improvement is difficult to bring about. For example, students of politics would agree that a short ballot, containing the names of only a few of the candidates for top office, is much to be preferred to a long ballot, containing a score of names of candidates for unimportant as well as important offices—at least, more than the typical voter has the time and opportunity to investigate intelligently. When a change to the short ballot is proposed, the opponents, who are usually working in the interests of the political machine, immediately raise the cry that this violates a basic principle of democracy—the public should have the right to vote for every office—even though selection through civil service could easily be undertaken. The result of this conscious effort to confuse is: no change. This same confusion between means and ends leads to a system of government that becomes so locked into a set of rigid forms that the result, all too often, is to defeat the very ends the opponents claim they are trying to protect.

A second source of resistance to change is the commonly accepted belief that the practices and forms now widely followed were adopted in the beginning only after long and careful study. The truth is usually the opposite. If one takes the trouble to investigate the origins of most of the forms and practices now slavishly followed, he will discover that many were instituted originally as a result of accident, compromise, or pure expediency. Such illegitimate beginnings do not rule them out, but no one should make the mistake of presuming that they were thought out carefully before they were adopted.

Even those forms and practices that have fully established their usefulness should be examined constantly to determine whether the passage of time does not require some change or modification. Many of the great failures in the business world—and in military campaigns—can be charged to the human tendency to apply too long a formula that has proved highly successful in the past.

A third source of resistance to change arises out of simple self-interest. A candidate who has won election to office cannot be expected to show much enthusiasm for changing the system. Of course, the same observation applies to persons in all walks of life. Those who have won success under the present rules are never eager to see a change in the rules; in fact, they will usually do everything in their power to retain them no matter how faulty they may be. This explains why it is extremely difficult to get members of Congress and of other legislative bodies to support any change or improvement in the electoral process, no matter how obvious the need is shown to be.

Nothing, for example, is so deeply rooted in democratic thinking as the idea that each citizen is entitled to one vote and to equal representation. Multiple votes are abhorrent. Yet until the Supreme Court took a hand in reapportionment, every state in the union had let itself drift into a situation in which some voters carried far more weight in legislative matters than did other voters in the same state. In fact, until the Supreme Court acted, a minority of voters in every state exercised control of their state legislatures. If changing this system had been left to the state legislatures, little would have been done, as experience of the past has proved. Self-interest too often overrides democratic principles.

A fourth source of resistance springs from nothing more than mental laziness of several varieties. Unless inspired or challenged, many persons go through life without expending any effort to get out of their well-worn mental ruts. Many, in fact, will go to almost any length to escape using their higher brain centers.

Like all the activities in which man engages, thinking can be work or it can be fun. Reading a book, discussing an important issue of the day, visiting a museum—even riding horseback—can be work or it can be fun, depending upon one's point of view. The tragedy of modern man is that thinking is not widely regarded as one of the pleasures of life, as it was at one stage in early history.

To be included in this same category of the mentally slothful are those persons who belong to the let-well-enough-alone school. These persons usually explain their avoidance of any mental exertion by the pretext that whatever exists is good enough. Somewhat akin to these persons are those who regard almost any problem as vastly more abstruse than it actually is. They wish to avoid the mental exertion of reducing complex problems to their simple components, rationalizing their laziness by warnings against oversimplification.

There is always the danger of oversimplifying. However, while the tendency of the mentally lazy to look for one cause when many are present should be guarded against, there is a like danger in the modern tendency to overcomplicate. Many scholars in many disciplines resort to ponderous scientific jargon to create the impression that they are privy to covert knowledge, which the layman could scarcely ever hope to comprehend. Simple matters are made to look exceedingly complex. There is a corresponding lack of interest in making complex matters simple.

Preparing for Change

Even though resistance to change springs from many sources, it is possible to overcome it in some instances, modify it in others. The fact that Western man actually courts change in some areas of life provides evidence that resistance to change is not inherent in his thinking. There is the further comforting thought: *In the whole history of man, no generation has been taught to expect change, to be prepared for change, or to seek change.*

The importance of preparing the individual for change has never been fully understood; nor has the importance of change in the advancement of society been fully recognized. If each new generation is to be indoctrinated with its importance, then the reasons for change must be more fully appreciated.

One of the most cogent reasons for accepting change concerns the mental health of the individual. In a highly complex society with its many anxiety-inducing factors, mental illness often results from the inability to adapt readily to new situations. On the other hand, proof that acceptance of change contributes to mental health—and to long life—has already been offered. The centenarians and nonagenarians investigated displayed a remarkable ability to accept change without mental disturbance. They took change in their stride.

The importance of being prepared for change can be illustrated by three situations arising during periods of war. The first example comes from World War II and has to do with the calm and collected manner in which the residents of London and other cities of Great Britain endured the bombings to which they were subjected almost nightly. Residents of these cities amazed the world by refusing to become nervous wrecks as a result of these daily brushes with death. They had prepared themselves for such an ordeal, and had adjusted their lives and their thinking accordingly.

In another war situation, lack of this mental resiliency and adaptability ended in disaster. The American soldiers who were taken prisoner by the Communists in the Korean War were unprepared for what might happen to them in the event that they fell into the hands of the enemy and were subjected to many kinds of torment, physical and mental. They had not been conditioned to meet such a situation; and as a result, many literally crumbled mentally and physically and died in shocking numbers. It was not their special weakness that brought about this collapse; other Americans of their age would have fallen apart as rapidly. It was the lack of proper instruction. They had not been conditioned to accept change.

By way of contrast, the Jews who were sent to Nazi concentration camps had steeled themselves to the awful horrors that they knew, or suspected, were in store for them. They gave a remarkable demonstration of how man can adjust to even the most cruel and inhuman torture when he is mentally prepared.

Since mental health has an important bearing upon physical health, conditioning the individual to embrace change is reason enough for making an effort to orient each new generation to expect and to welcome it. Even more important, only through change of a drastic order will man begin to actualize his potentialities. The opportunities that lie ahead in the fuller employment of brain power cannot be realized if man chains himself to the *status quo.*

The driving force for change and for making better use of man's mental abilities must come from the public, not from its leaders. This may seem unusual, until it is recognized that much of the opposition to change comes from the very persons who might be expected to advocate it most vigorously.

The field of education offers a good example. If major changes are to take place in the educational system, the movement is not likely to be led by educators. Persons who have struggled through a long period of training in a particular field and who have subsequently established themselves in positions of leadership cannot be expected to fight very hard for changing the system, no matter what its shortcomings. Educators are not alone in this failing. The same principle applies to militarists, journalists, businessmen, diplomats, doctors, lawyers, politicians, and those engaged in any profession or calling where much training is required and positions of authority and leadership are hard to achieve.

The penalties for instituting—or even advocating—change can be severe. Leaders risk their positions of leadership. Moreover, change of any kind requires a certain amount of readjustment, and if the change is great, it can require much time and effort spent in relearning. The leader who advocates radical change is almost certain to incur the wrath of other leaders in his field, and of the rank and file as well. Witness the educators, militarists, and medical practitioners who have fought for important and needed changes in their fields, only to reap a harvest of scorn from their co-workers.

Society must recognize that as a result of these pressures, change cannot be brought about easily by its leaders, except in those situations in which the changes advocated do not disturb present relationships. In fact, it is the leaders who typically become the most bitter and the most effective foes of change. The public, therefore, must take the initiative and assume responsibility for progress in the affairs of man. *The public must force change upon its leaders.*

Unfortunately, the public cannot look to experts or specialists, for the very same reasons that it cannot expect change to be initiated by its leaders. With the trend toward greater specialization, the expert and specialist command more respect today than they perhaps deserve. The expert merits respect for his special knowledge; but like the leader, he is expert in his small world as it presently exists, not expert in the world as it might be. Although he plays an important role in modern society, it is not realistic to expect him to advocate drastic change. This is the surest way for him to lose his status of expert.

Any intrusion into these special fields by laymen is likely to be resented by expert and leader alike. For this reason, the layman must be prepared to accept abuse and ridicule. The expert will do everything he can to keep the layman at a distance. One stratagem has been found effective in countering any new idea offered by an outsider. Henry George described it this way: "The first thing they say is that it isn't true. And when its truth can no longer be denied, they say it isn't important. And when its importance is firmly established, they say it isn't new."

The hope of the future rests with the citizen. To be effective, he must be well informed, and he must discover ways of making better use of his own great mental capacities and those of his fellow men. He cannot expect his leaders to give him much help in his upward march. Woodrow Wilson expressed the thought this way when he said, "The great struggling unknown masses . . . are the dynamic force that is lifting the levels of society. A nation is as great, and only as great, as her rank and file."

Conclusion

Can man perform the miracle of lifting himself to a higher level of civilization?

The answer is Yes—unequivocally. Man is clearly in charge of his own evolution; he can proceed at a pace that he himself sets.

He can solve any problem that comes within his purview—even the problem of war. The great advances made in physical science can be paralleled in social science. Man now has the procedures for dealing with the problems arising out of his social existence—problems that the methods of physical science cannot adequately explore or illuminate.

Man has scarcely begun to make use of his almost limitless brain power, either individually or collectively. Lack of progress in dealing with the affairs of mankind can be traced to a simple truth: man has never made a concerted and persistent effort to solve his social and political problems. His inventive genius has been confined almost exclusively to the production of better tools and instruments.

The next great move forward can now be taken. All that is required is a firm belief in man's great potentialities and a readiness to accept change.

Man is still young on the face of the earth; civilization is still in its infancy. *Homo sapiens* has not yet realized his strength and his greatness; nor does he see, except dimly, the heights to which civilization can reach.

Three hundred years ago it was equally difficult to foresee the great advances in science that the future held in store. Only Francis Bacon had that vision. He also had a vision of man with which this book might properly close: "Men are not animals erect but immortal gods."

Bibliography

N. J. BERRILL, *Man's Emerging Mind,* Dodd, Mead & Co.

LE GROS CLARK, *History of the Primates,* British Museum.

COOKIE and ROBINSON, *Royal Commissions of Inquiry,* Stanford University Press.

JOHN D. DAVIES, *Phrenology—Fad and Science,* Yale University Press.

GEORGE GALLUP and EVAN HILL, *Secrets of Long Life,* Bernard Geis Associates.

DR. RALPH WALDO GERARD, *An Outline of Man's Knowledge of the Modern World,* Nelson Doubleday.

GEN. LESLIE R. GROVES, *Now It Can Be Told,* Harper & Brothers.

ALDOUS HUXLEY, *Control of the Mind,* McGraw-Hill.

SIR RICHARD LIVINGSTONE, *On Education,* Macmillan.

PIERRE TEILHARD DE CHARDIN, *The Phenomenon of Man,* Harper & Brothers.

W. GREY WALTER, *The Living Brain,* Duckworth.

ABOUT THE AUTHOR

George Gallup's name is associated with public opinion polls throughout the world; a lesser-known side of Dr. Gallup is his interest in people and the factors which influence their opinions, attitudes, and aspirations.

Born in Jefferson, Iowa, he attended the University of Iowa and spent ten years as a teacher there and at Drake, Northwestern, and Columbia universities. He has always had a great interest in education.

Another major interest is local government. He is a former president of the National Municipal League, and during the past twelve years has served as chairman of a jury which selects All-America cities on the basis of intelligent and effective citizen activity.

Dr. Gallup's research activities cover the fields of health, religion, politics, journalism, advertising, entertainment, education, and philosophy. It can be said that no other person has had the opportunity to study the views of so many people on so many aspects of modern life, and in so many parts of the world.

Dr. Gallup and his wife live in Princeton, New Jersey.

Format by SIDNEY FEINBERG
Set in Linotype Baskerville
Composed, printed and bound by American Book-Stratford Press, Inc.
HARPER & ROW, PUBLISHERS, INCORPORATED